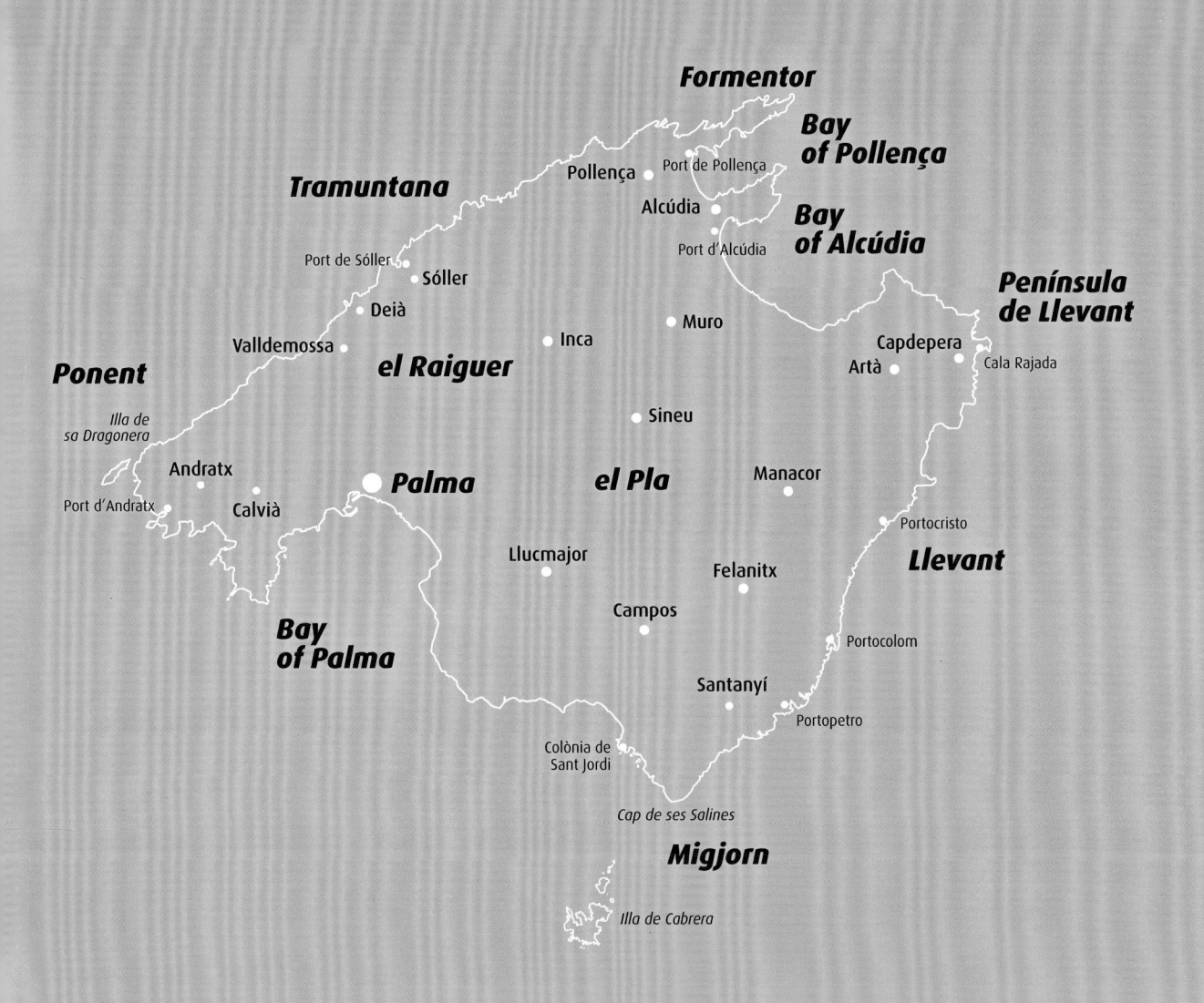

Mallorca

Tramuntana
Formentor
Pollença
Port de Pollença
Bay of Pollença
Alcúdia
Port d'Alcúdia
Bay of Alcúdia
Port de Sóller
Sóller
Deià
Valldemossa
Muro
Capdepera
Península de Llevant
Artà
Cala Rajada

Ponent
Illa de sa Dragonera
el Raiguer
Inca
Sineu
Andratx
Port d'Andratx
Calvià
Palma
el Pla
Manacor
Portocristo
Llevant
Llucmajor
Felanitx
Portocolom
Bay of Palma
Campos
Santanyí
Portopetro
Colònia de Sant Jordi
Cap de ses Salines
Migjorn
Illa de Cabrera

Triangle ▸ Books

Mallorca

Viewpoint of Sa Creueta or des Colomer, Formentor

Contents

An island is always a recreation of paradise, but, on Mallorca, several of them come together on a single land mass: sands bathed by turquoise waters, coves nestling between the cliffs, mountains criss-crossed by coal miners' paths, natural spaces where birds thrive and an inland plateau dotted with villages which are steeped in tradition and where tranquillity reins.

Palma p. 4 | **The Bay of Palma** p. 28 | **Ponent** p. 36 | **Tramuntana** p. 46 | **Formentor** p. 68 | **The bays of Pollença and Alcúdia** p. 74 | **Península de Llevant** p. 88 | **Llevant** p. 100 | **Migjorn** p. 110 | **The interior** p. 124 | **Gastronomy** p. 138 | **Handicrafts** p. 140 | **Traditions** p. 142

Palma

The cathedral and L'Almudaina from the Parc de la Mar

Palma

With more than 400,000 inhabitants, the capital of Mallorca is a city on a human scale overlooking the Mediterranean. Situated in the middle of a vast bay with the imposing Gothic cathedral as it focal point, it has an old town dotted with elegant mansions with shady courtyards. Throughout the year, it offers a whole host of cultural, retail and culinary attractions and, every day, the local markets receive fresh produce from the land and sea around the island. A long promenade, which is popular with walkers and sports lovers who enjoy the urban beaches, follows from the bay, where you can see the outline of boats heading inland on the horizon.

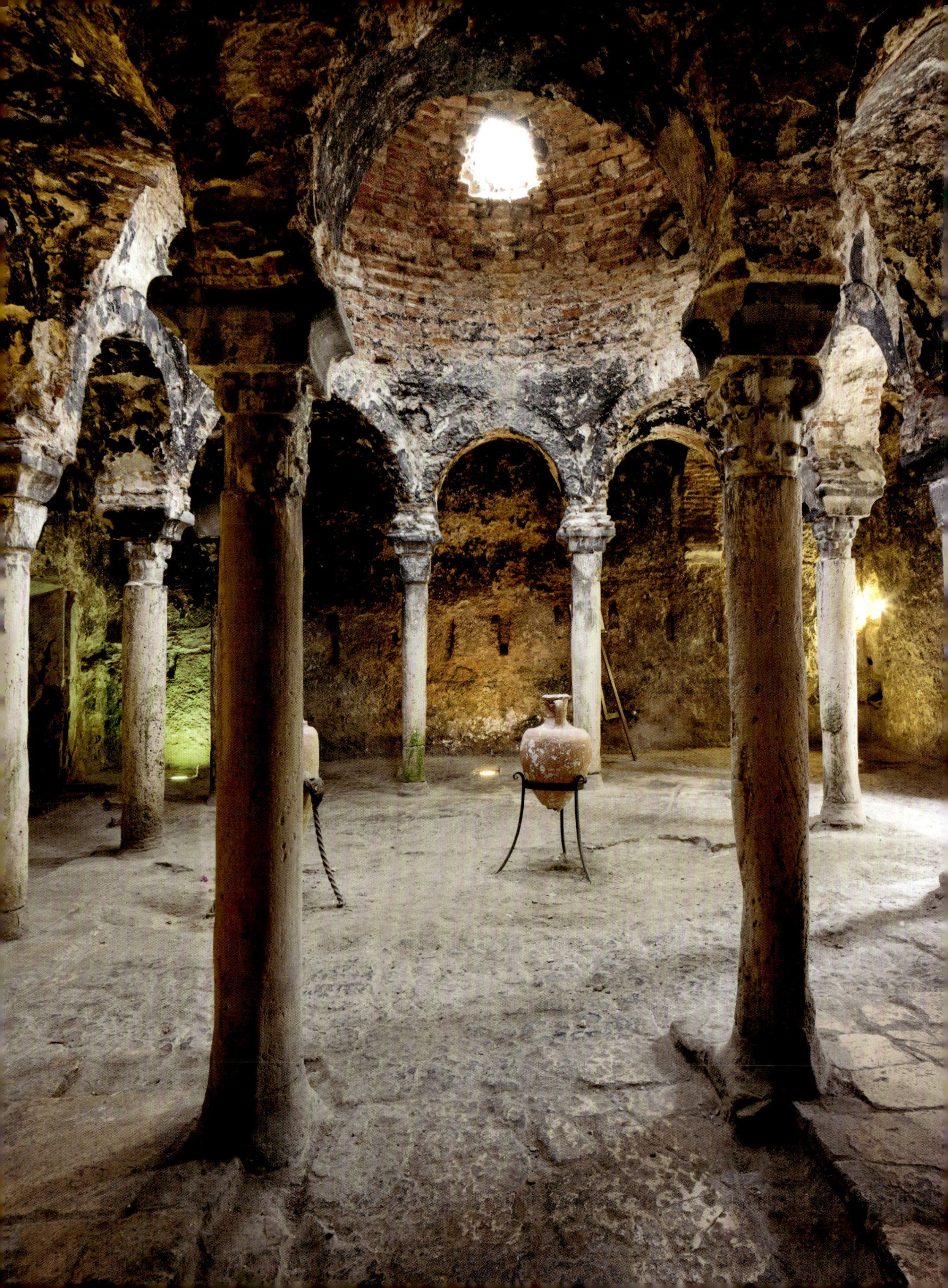

Palma

The old town
The old town of Palma spans the Passeig del Born. Behind the cathedral, a network of narrow lanes makes up the old Ciutat Alta, which has a profusion of palaces built from the 16th century onwards by the nobility and thriving middle classes. They were subsequently refurbished according to the tastes of their owners. The old Ciutat Baixa is located to the right of the Born, and is also home to important mansions. It is a portside district whose life centres around the boatyards and the place where the chandlers had their premises in olden times.

The Arab Baths
The Arab conquest of Mallorca took place in 903 AD and Palma was transformed into Madina Mayurqa, a splendid city of which few traces remain. The Arab Baths are most important surviving feature. They date from the 10th and 11th centuries and consist of a central chamber with 12 columns, horseshoe arches and a semi-spherical dome where people would take hot baths and an adjacent room with a rectangular floor plan. On the ground you can still see the marks left by the water pipes, some of them connected to a water wheel in the garden. Elements from earlier periods, such as capitals, were used to build the baths.

Jaume I
Between 1229 and 1231 the Catalan king Jaume I seized Mallorca from the Arabs: the old Madina Mayurqa, which is today known as Palma, fell in December 1229 but the Muslim resistance became entrenched in the mountains where the battle went on for three more years. The Christian troops disembarked on the coast of Santa Ponça in September 1229 and, following the conquest, and as described in the book known as the *Llibre del Repartiment*, the king shared out the island's territories among the nobles who had accompanied him on his campaign. Jaume I set up a strategic enclave for international trade in the Kingdom of Mallorca, which was independent from the Crown of Aragon.

← The Arab Baths

The gate of L'Almudaina

King Jaume I

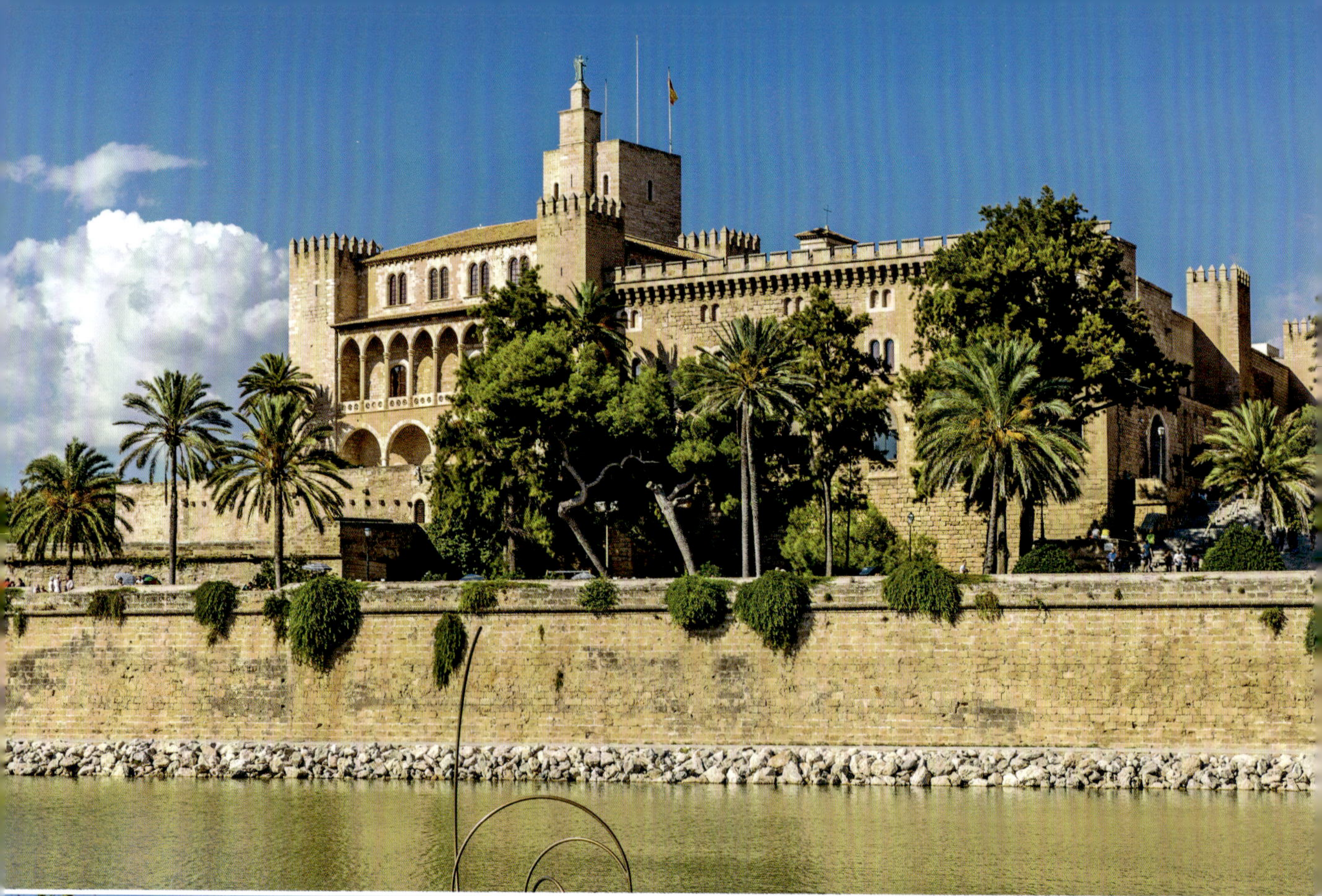

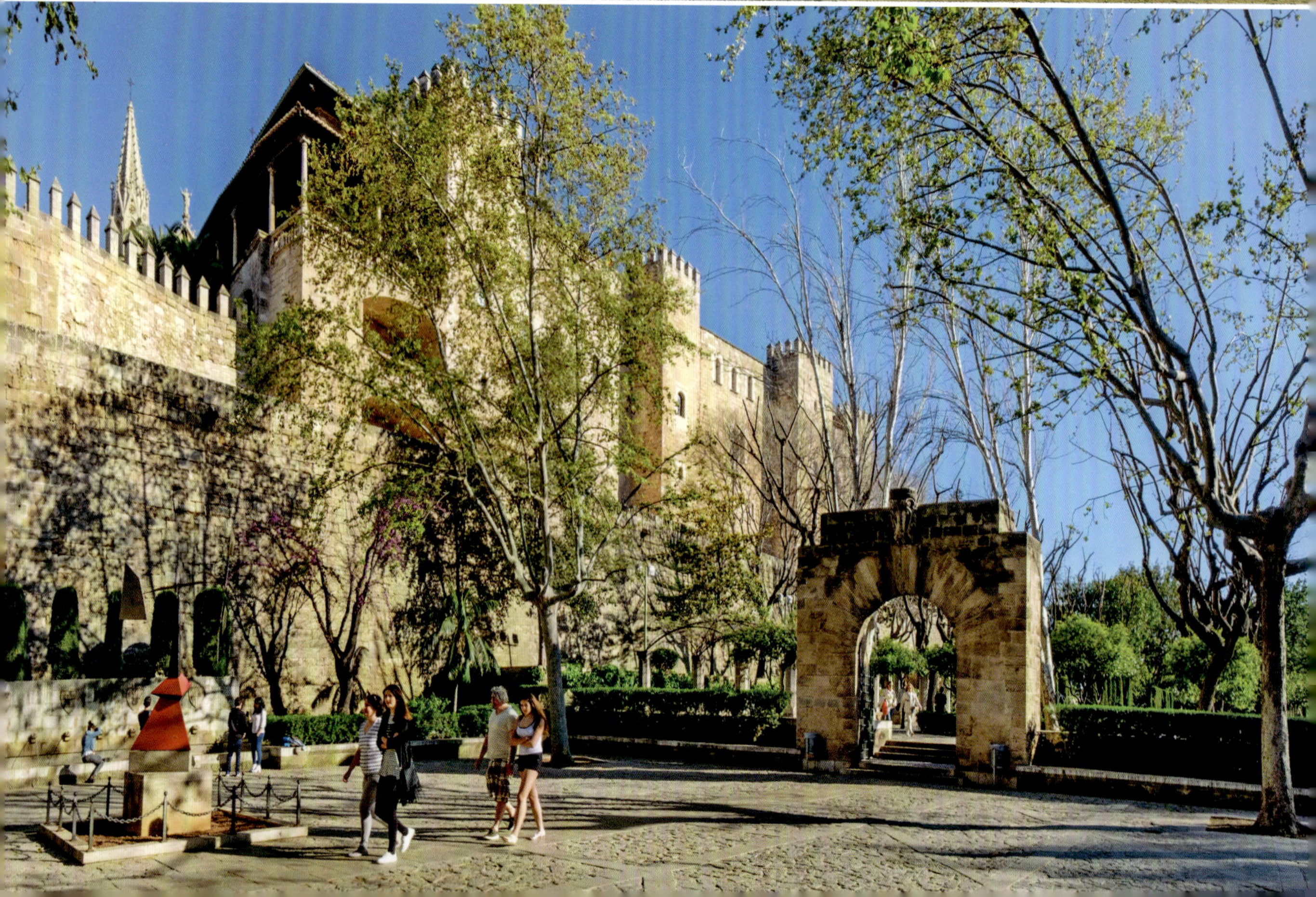

Palma

L'Almudaina
Dwarfed by the vast cathedral, this Arabian fortress retains the traces of much of Palma's history. Built on Roman remains and home to the governor, or wali, it was first recorded in written documents in the 12th and 13th centuries. The Christian conquerors built the Royal Palace of L'Almudaina for King Jaume II on the site between 1305 and 1314. It flourished as the main court of his successors, the kings of Mallorca, Sanç I and Jaume III. Highlights include the Royal Chapel of Santa Anna, the Great Hall, or Tinell, and the King's Palace, the Palau del Rei. Significant renovations was carried out at the beginning of the 20th century, followed by further restorations. The palace was built on a rectangular floor plan and is enclosed by walls flanked by square towers. One of the most important is the Torre de l'Homenatge, also known as the Torre de l'Àngel, which is surmounted by a sculpture dating from the early 14th century representing the archangel Gabriel.

S'Hort des Rei
This landscaped area, with its pergolas, water fountains and sculptures by artists including Alexander Calder and Joan Miró stretches out at the foot of L'Almudaina. It used to be the Royal Palace garden, where cypresses, palms, vines, vegetables and orange and lemon trees once grew.

Sa Llotja
A masterpiece of civilian Gothic architecture designed Guillem Sagrera to house the headquarters of the Merchants' Stock Exchange, the Col·legi de la Mercaderia. This institution was founded in the early 15th century and was in charge of regulating and protecting trade and also for the upkeep of the port. Inside, six slender columns rise up to the high ceiling where they fan out like palm trees forming ribbed vaults. Sa Llotja now hosts art exhibitions.

S'Hort des Rei

Sa Llotja

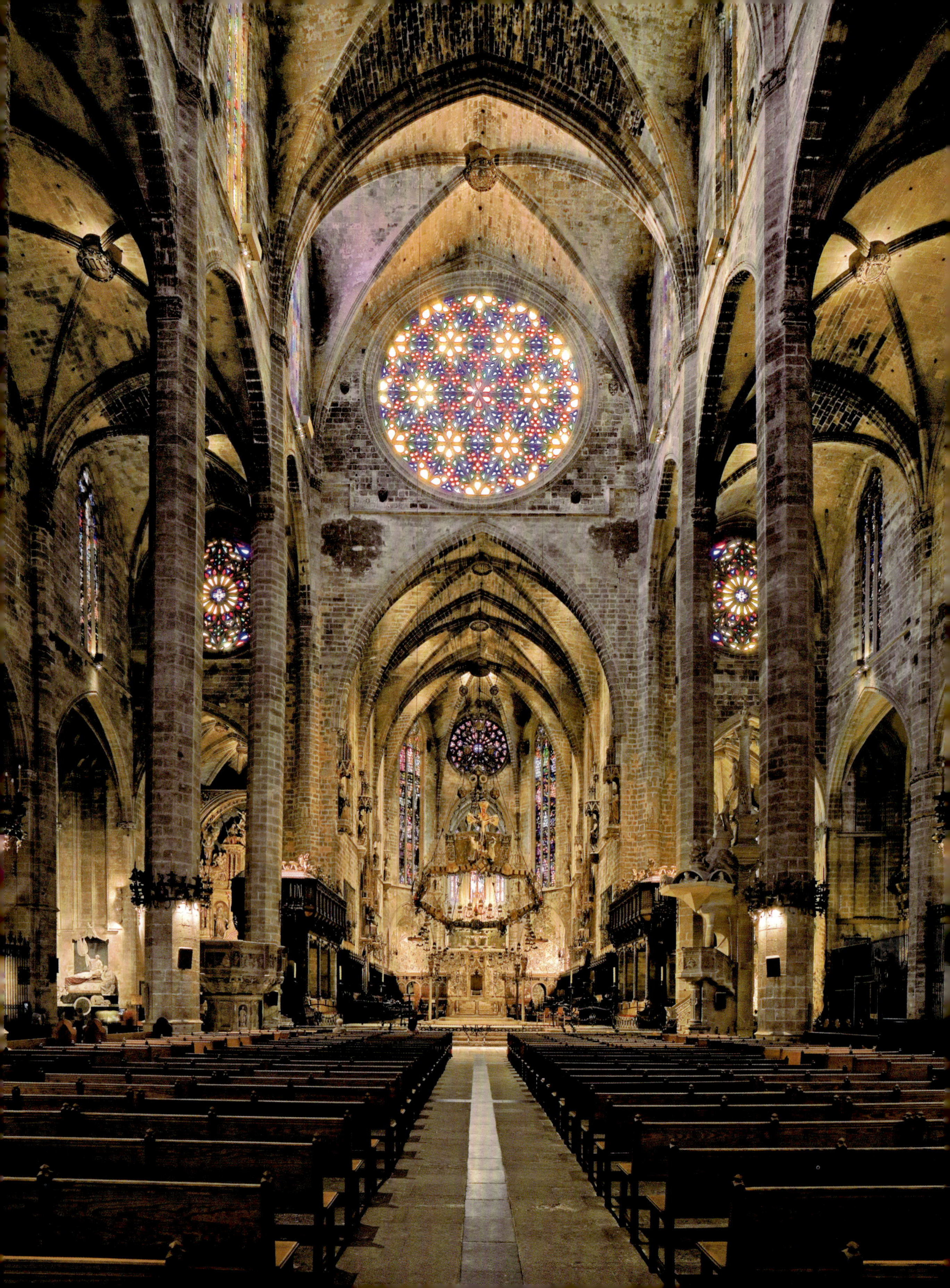

Palma

The cathedral of Santa Maria, a space of light

In the middle of the bay, the cathedral towers over the city's seafront and is one of its major landmarks. According to legend, the Christian ships that were heading to conquer Mallorca in 1229 were caught in a violent storm. It is said that King Jaume I prayed to the Virgin promising that he would build a church in her honour if he survived. He stayed true to his word and the cathedral was built on the site of a mosque which was demolished in 1386 but used as a Christian place of worship in the interim.

Work on the cathedral wasn't completed until 1601. Built of sandstone from quarries on Mallorca, its interior space and light make it particularly stunning. It is divided into three naves with eight chapels on each side. It covers an area of 6,600 m² and has 83 stained-glass windows and seven rose windows. The largest rose window, known as the "Gothic Eye", stands 30 m above the central apse. It covers an area of almost 100 m² and is the largest Gothic window of its kind. It consists of 24 triangles, half of which make up the Star of David. Twice a year, on 11th November and 2nd February, the light from the rose window is projected onto the main façade. A magical moment which hundreds of people flock to see.

Outside, the belfry, which stands 48 m high, forms an angle with the doorway of L'Almoina. It was probably built on the base of the minaret from the former mosque. Work on the tower concluded at the end of the 15th century and to reach the top you have to climb a spiral staircase with 215 steps. The walls still bear graffiti made by people seeking sanctuary in the cathedral. Right at the top are the nine cathedral bells. Particularly impressive is the bell known as N'Eloi, which is 2 m in diameter.

Winter Solstice

Antoni Gaudí's intervention

With the passing centuries, the architectural value of the cathedral has been enriched with interventions in different styles. One of the most important was the restoration carried out by the Catalan architect, Antoni Gaudí, between 1904 and 1924, at the behest of the bishop Pere Joan Campins Barceló. Gaudí transformed the interior of the cathedral: he moved the choir stalls from the centre of the nave to the sides by splitting them into two sections. This intervention was criticised at the time. He took down the altarpieces and a gallery in the presbytery to gain greater visual perspective during services.

He also placed a new canopy over the high altar consisting of a seven-sided ring and 35 lamps. It was never completed. The one you see today is actually a model of the final project. He created a new pulpit to the left of the high altar and introduced wrought-iron elements inspired by the art nouveau movement. These included railings and candelabras placed on the pillars underpinning the central nave.

Gaudí worked on the project with the architects Joan Rubió i Bellver and Josep Maria Jujol, the sculptor Vicenç Villarrubias and the painters Joaquín Torres García, Iu Pascual and Jaume Llongueras. These interventions were never completed.

Detail of the choir stalls by Jujol

Detail of the cathedral canopy by Gaudí

Miquel Barceló's ceramic skin

The Mallorcan artist Miquel Barceló carried out one of the most rewarding interventions inside the cathedral, or La Seu as it is known locally. It was placed inside Saint Peter's chapel in 2006. The chapel is in the right-hand apse in the eastern end of the cathedral. The installation consists of a multicoloured-ceramic mural measuring some 300 m² which covers almost all the chapel walls. It also includes five darkened stained-glass windows which stand 12 m high and furniture created with stone from Binissalem —altar, ambo, presidential chair and two benches—.

Barceló's installation recreates the iconography of Jesus multiplying the loaves and fishes and the wedding of Cana with a ceramic triptych featuring allegories to the sea, land and humanity. On the right, the sea is depicted as a giant wave with seaweed, octopuses, sea bass, mussels and skate; on the left, the land is recreated with bread, wine vats, fruit and vegetables. The central section features a representation of Christ while the grey light that enters through the stained-glass windows recreates the atmosphere of the sea.

Miquel Barceló's intervention was promoted by Bishop Teodor Úbeda with the support of the bodies that are part of the Art a la Seu Foundation.

Detail of the ceramic skin

Bread, wine, fruits of the earth on Miquel Barceló's mural

Es Baluard

Es Baluard Museu d'Art Modern i Contemporani is situated within the perimeter of the Sant Pere bastion which is part of the Renaissance wall that encircled the city of Palma until the beginning of the 20th century. The museum building covers a surface area of more than 5,000 m² and is defined by simple, clean lines. It was designed by the architects Lluís García-Ruiz, Jaume García-Ruiz, Vicente Tomás and Ángel Sánchez Cantalejo and the permanent collection brings together works by artists and movements that have converged on the Balearic Islands since the beginning of the last century: painters from the Catalan art nouveau, or *modernista*, movement —Joaquim Mir, Santiago Rusiñol, Hermen Anglada-Camarasa and Joaquín Sorolla— the avant-garde and other movements from the middle of the 20th century —Pablo Picasso, Joan Miró and Wifredo Lam— and contemporary art trends.

Es Baluard

Puig de Sant Pere

Palma

Puig de Sant Pere
The district of Puig de Sant Pere is located behind the Plaça de la Drassana, the former site of the shipyards. Its focal point is the Gothic church of Santa Creu, which houses the beautiful crypt of Sant Llorenç, a small oratory with five chapels built between the 13th and 14th centuries.

Sa Calatrava
This former fishing quarter stretches out behind the Parc de la Mar on the right of the cathedral. It is packed with charming spots such as the tiny Plaça de Sant Jeroni. It also is home to the main galleries of the island's museum, the Museu de Mallorca, which is housed in a palace known as Ca la Gran Cristiana. This building stands on the foundations of two Gothic mansions and retains part of the original baroque pentagonal structure.

Carrer Can Savellà

Plaça Sant Jeroni

The courtyards

A walk along the narrow lanes in the old town, particularly those around the cathedral, allows us to glimpse inside the courtyards of the mansions that belonged to Mallorca's old nobility and middle classes. Shady places, protected from the rain, where, in times past, their owners, servants and neighbours would come and go, children would play, and carriages, horses and mules would draw up. Built in different styles, most of them were renovated in the 16th and 17th centuries, although some retain their original Gothic elements. Travellers, including Archduke Ludwig Salvator, George Sand and Frédéric Chopin, sung the praises of these unique architectural features.

Cal Marquès de Vivot (Can Vivot)

Palma

Churches and convents

The city has a profusion of religious buildings, many of them built by Jaume I following the Christian conquest in the 13th century. A number of churches were built on the site of mosques. One of them, Sant Miquel, is considered the oldest in Palma. Churches and convents are home to works of art from every genre. This is the case of the cloisters of the church of Sant Francesc, which were built between the 14th to the 17th centuries. Their slender columns and lobular arches demarcate a place of contemplation in the heart of the city. In the 19th century, the Mendizábal Disentailment Act confiscated 33 of the 44 convents on Mallorca, and some of them went into private ownership while others were simply demolished.

Cloisters of Sant Francesc

Convent of Santa Magdalena

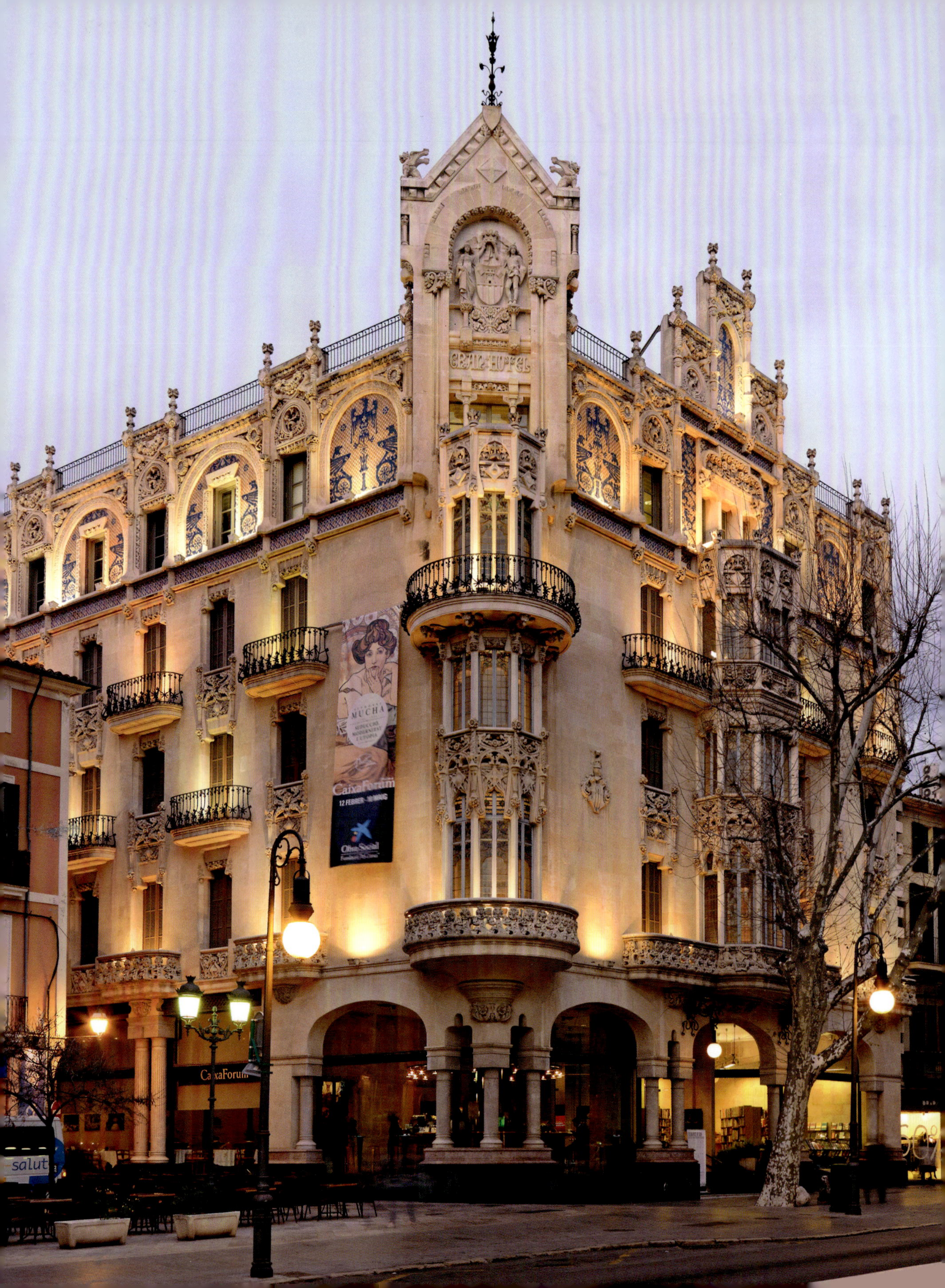
GRAN HOTEL
MUCHA
CaixaForum
CaixaForum
salut

Palma

Art-nouveau and *modernista* buildings

The turn of the 20th century brought with it a new way of thinking that placed its trust in progress and trade. Art nouveau was the artistic movement that embodied this fresh mindset. The ground-breaking genre, and its Catalan offshoot, *modernisme*, gave Palma buildings such as the Gran Hotel, which opened in 1903, and, a year later, brought the architect Antoni Gaudí to Mallorca where he had been commissioned to renovate the cathedral. The city has a vast array of buildings that reveal the influences of art nouveau and *modernisme* which can be seen in shops such as the Forn des Teatre and Forn Fondo.

However, the Gran Hotel is, without question, the most iconic turn-of-the-century building because it expresses a commitment to tourism as a driving force for the economy and business. Designed by the architect Lluís Domènech i Montaner, it was the first hotel on Mallorca to offer visitors all the comforts of a top-class establishment. The façade is decorated in lavish floral motifs, with wrought-iron elements and ceramic embellishments featuring eagles and dragons.

Other buildings in the same style can be found in the nearby Plaça del Mercat: Can Casasayas and the Pensión Menorquina, designed by the architects Francesc Roca and Simó y Guillem Reynés i Font and built between 1980 and 1911, make up a pigeon pair. The sandstone façades are imbued with a dynamic energy and have the typical Mallorcan shutters that adapt to the arches, and wrought-iron elements depicting ferns and butterflies.

Can Barceló, in the Plaça de Josep Maria Quadrado, is another beautiful example of *modernista* architecture, in this case applied to a detached family house built between 1902 and 1904 to a design by Bartomeu Ferrà i Perelló. The façade is decorated with ceramic panels depicting allegories of the arts, the textile industry and trade, while the balconies and windows reveal delicate wrought ironwork.

← Gran Hotel, headquarters of CaixaForum in Palma

Can Casasayas and Pensión Menorquina

Can Barceló

Plaça de Cort

This square is the hub of activity in Palma and home to Palma City Council and the government, the Consell de Mallorca. The Balearic Islands Parliament stands nearby. The Plaça de Cort links up with the Plaça de Santa Eulàlia and the Plaça Major and is packed with bars, restaurants and shops. In the Middle Ages, it was home to the scribes who worked for different jurisdictions and notaries, the curias, the prison and the hospital of Sant Andreu. Public auctions and executions were also held here. An ancient olive tree stands in the middle of the square, a symbol of peace and attachment to the land.

Palma City Hall

Consell Insular de Mallorca

Carrer de Joanot Colom

Square and church of Santa Eulàlia

A square which has the Gothic church of Santa Eulàlia as its centrepiece. This was one of the first churches built on Mallorca following the Christian conquest. It stands on the site of a mosque and hosted the coronation of King Jaume II, the son of Jaume I. The church has three naves, two doors and a slender 19th-century bell tower crowned by a pointed spire. Outside, there are gargoyles in the shape of dragons, harpies and basilisks.

Church of Santa Eulàlia

Palma

The Passeig des Born
A central boulevard which is one of the city's most popular spots where you can stroll and stop off at one of the pavement cafés. The word *born* is characteristic of the cities of the Crown of Aragon and referred to a wide, open space where games and tournaments were held. The sphinxes that stand guard along the boulevard were placed there in 1833 together with the fountain, the Font de la Princesa, which marks the entrance to Carrer de Jaume III.

Plaça Major
The shopping streets, such as Sant Miquel, Sindicat and Colom, lead off this wide, bustling, central square. Renovations in the 19th century destroyed the medieval layout along with buildings such as the Casa de l'Inquisició, which was also known as the *casa negra*, or "black house". A craft fair is held in the square throughout the year and, at Christmas, there are stalls selling the typical, brightly coloured Mallorcan Nativity figures made of clay.

La Rambla
The Riera torrent once flowed down this boulevard lined with flower and plant stalls. Today the central section is pedestrianised and there are traffic lanes on either side. The former charitable institution, La Misericòrdia, stands at one end. It currently houses local government offices, a library an exhibition centre and a contemporary-sculpture garden

The cathedral seen from the Passeig del Born

Plaça Major

Church of Sant Jaume

La Rambla

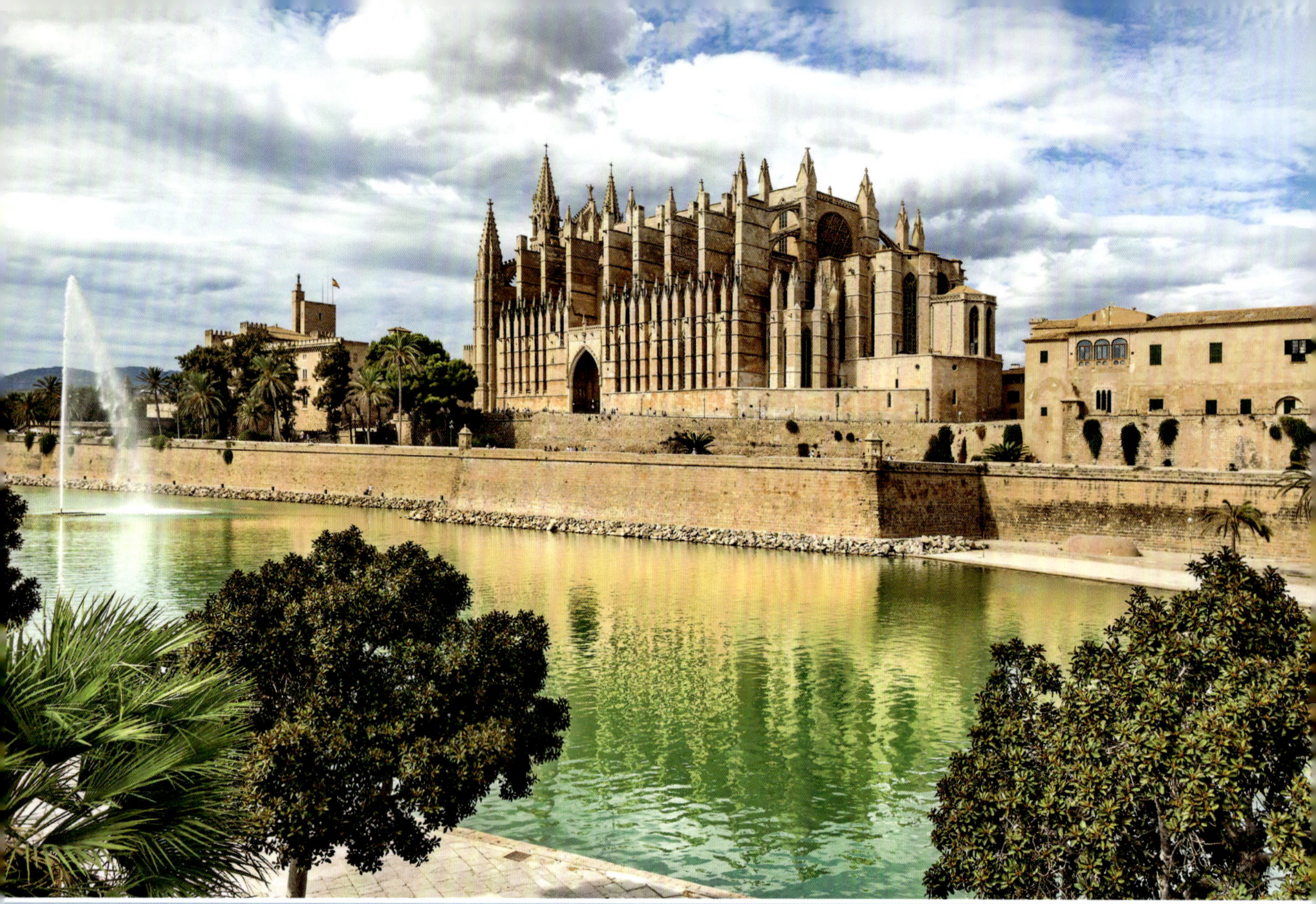

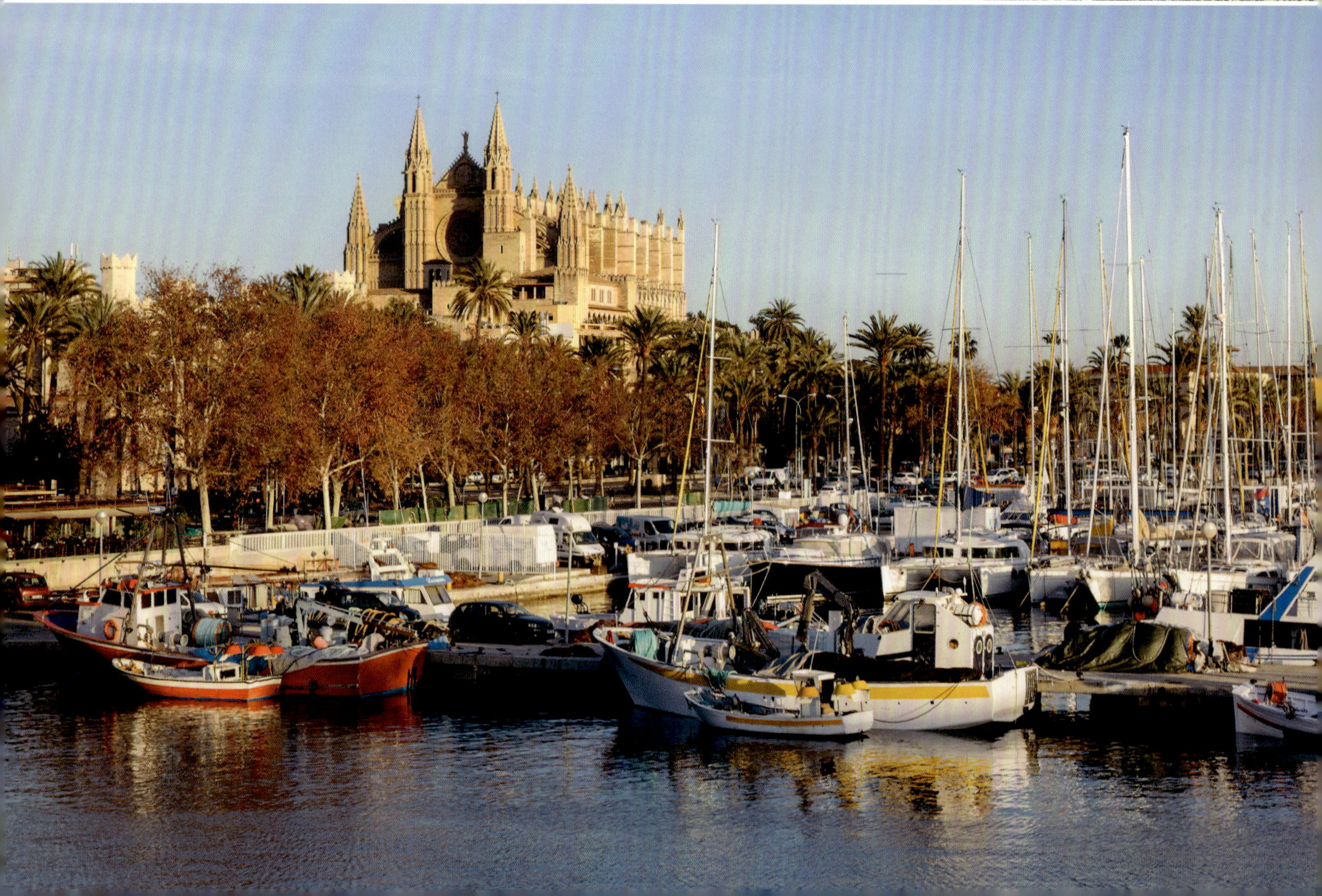

Palma

Parc de la Mar
This park lies below the cathedral. Covering an area of more than 68,000 m², it stands on land reclaimed from the sea. It follows the line of the old city walls and has a salt-water lake with a water jet in the middle, a green space and sculptures by artists including Alfons Sard and Josep Guinovart.

The harbour
A long promenade, built on land reclaimed from the sea, runs the entire length of Palma's bustling harbour. Take a leisurely stroll or bike ride to see the commercial docks, the fish quays and marinas where all kinds of vessels are moored, from luxury yachts to simple Mediterranean sailing boats, known as *llaüts*.

Es Jonquet
The windmills in this fishing quarter are an integral part of the skyline and have been used as locations for films like *Blackjack* (1950). Standing on the edge of the Santa Catalina district, Es Jonquet consists of a network of short streets and low-built houses painted in different colours. It is known for its laid-back pace of life.

Santa Catalina
A historic fishing quarter which is now the place where young foreigners choose to live. They bring a cosmopolitan vibe to this area with its thriving restaurant scene featuring cuisine from around the world. The top chefs shop at the Santa Catalina Market with its plentiful array of fresh fish, seafood, fruit and vegetables.

Es Jonquet

Santa Catalina

Palma harbour

24 ASSORTED COLORS
MONGOL
EXTRA STRONG
THIN LEAD PENCILS
CAN BE SHARPENED TO A NEEDLE POINT

Land of Miró

Joan Miró lived on Mallorca and had his studio in Cala Major which you can see when you visit the Fundació Pilar i Joan Miró. He worked there from 1956 until his death. The studio still contains the paintbrushes, canvases and personal items that offer a remarkable insight into Miró's creative environment. The foundation also has a building designed by the architect Rafael Moneo where a selection of Miró's work is on display.

Miró had close ties with Mallorca: his mother was Mallorcan and, in 1929, he married Pilar Juncosa who also hailed from the island. He moved to Mallorca in 1940 fleeing the German bombing raids and lived there for two years. He made his permanent home in Palma in 1954 where he built a studio designed by the architect Josep Lluís Sert. Five years later he bought Son Boter —an 18th century house adjacent to his studio— which he used as an extra workshop, painting and drawing on the walls.

In later life, Miró continued to create sculptures, works on paper, ceramics, murals, stained-glass windows, tapestries, stage sets and costumes for the theatre. He died on Christmas Day 1983 at his home Son Abrines, in Palma.

Son Boter

Bellver Castle

Perched on a wooded hill, more than 100 m above the city, Bellver Castle was built between 1300 and 1311 at the behest of the king of Mallorca, Jaume II. It is a Gothic building with a circular ground plan with four towers placed on the cardinal points of the compass. One of them is separated from the rest and was used as the last bastion of resistance in the case of an enemy attack.

The castle occupies a strategic position: from the top of the hill the occupants could watch for any threats from land or sea. Although, on the outside, the castle resembled a fortress, on the inside it was a refined and elegant palace. The rooms on the ground floor were used to store provisions, while the mezzanine housed the royal family's chambers, reception rooms and a chapel.

Following the War of the Spanish Succession (1700-1715) the castle was used as a prison and eminent personalities were held there, including the intellectual Gaspar Melchor de Jovellanos and the astronomer and politician François Arago. During the Spanish Civil War (1936-1939) hundreds of republicans who had defended the legally elected government were imprisoned in Bellver. The castle is now home to the city's history museum, the Museu d'Història de la Ciutat and part of the art collection of Cardinal Despuig.

Bellver forest

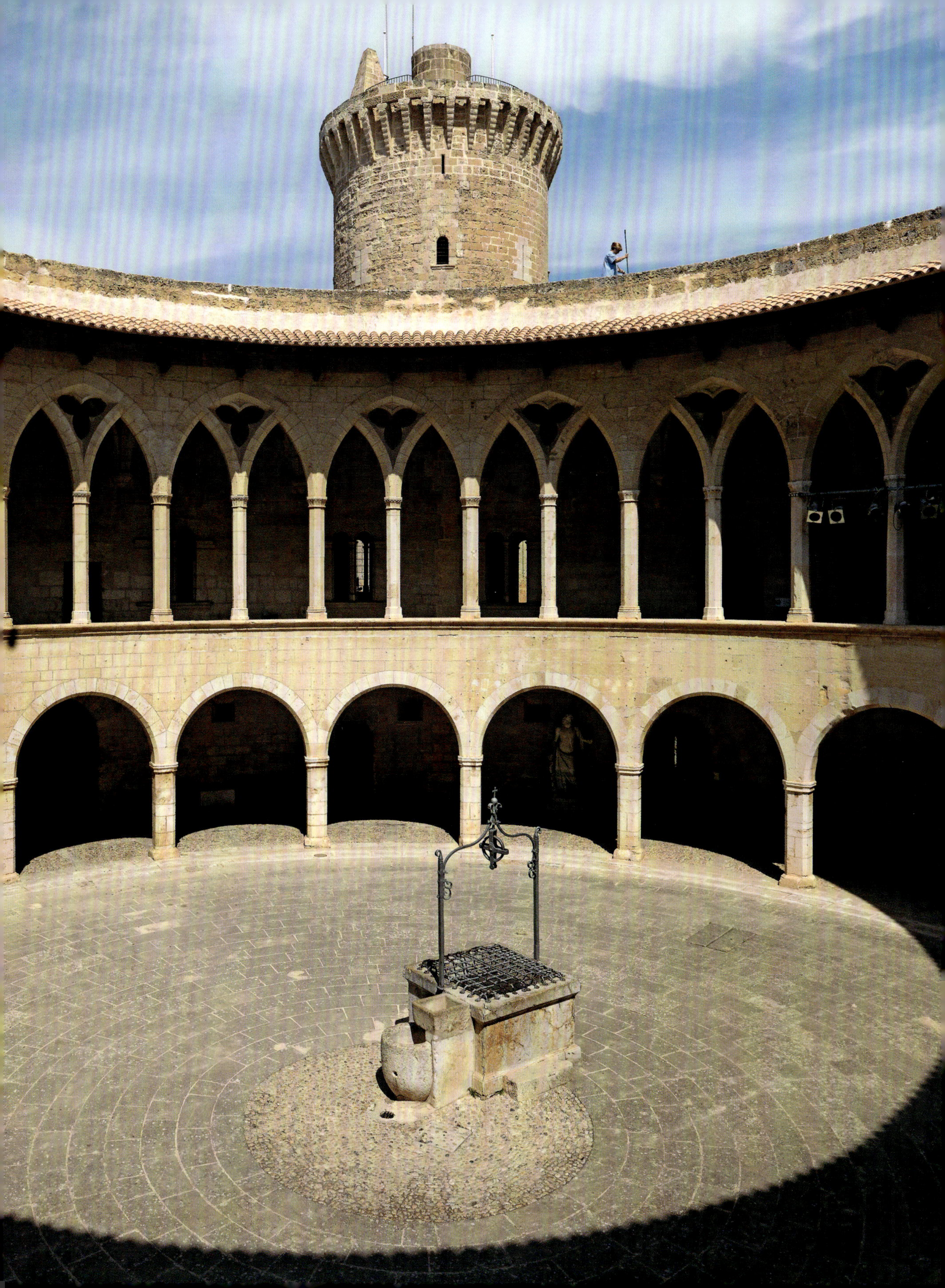

The Bay of Palma

Coast of Magaluf and islet of Sa Porrassa

The Bay of Palma

The vast bay has the Palma seafront as its centrepiece. At each end are the sandy urban beaches that have good transport links with the city. The fishing districts of Es Portitxol and Es Molinar overlook the sea, and, behind them are the residential neighbourhoods and resorts such as Can Pastilla and S'Arenal. Stretching to the west are the sands of Illetes, Palmanova, Magaluf, Portals Vells and Santa Ponça, the summer destinations of thousands of European tourists who go there in search of boisterous nightlife and relaxation in equal measure. In winter, the almost-deserted beaches become a haven of peace frequented by walkers, sporty types and seasoned swimmers.

Can Pere Antoni, Es Portitxol and Es Molinar

Can Pere Antoni beach has views of Mallorca Cathedral. It is the epitome of the urban beach, can be reached on foot from the centre of Palma, and is enjoyed all the year round by people who do sport or like walking by the sea. The promenade runs along the beach and a bike lane to the east, leads to the districts of Es Portitxol and Es Molinar, where several flour mills once stood. The ancient fishing enclaves, with their low-build houses, painted in different colours, still retain the feel of traditional fishing villages due to the small harbours where the Mediterranean sailing boats, known as *llaüts*, are moored.

Es Portitxol

Waterfront

The Bay of Palma

Platja de Palma and S'Arenal

Residential neighbourhoods and tourist resorts have developed around an idyllic and uninterrupted strip of sand. In summer they are a magnet for families with children and young people from Europe who come here in search of fun and entertainment. S'Arenal was originally a fishing village where wealthy families from Palma built their summer homes in the late 19th century, and building work commenced on the church dedicated to Our Lady of the Milk, the Mare de Déu de la Lactància. At the time the vast beach was surrounded by pine glades, savin junipers, wild olive trees and dune flora. Tourism began in the 1950s bringing with it a marked growth in the population —particularly workers from mainland Spain— and the first hotels opened.

Calvià

A popular tourist area. Its beaches include Illetes, Portals Nous, Palmanova and Portals Vells, which overlook the Bay of Palma, and El Toro, Santa Ponça and Peguera which face west. Although its coastline is synonymous with crowds in summer, life is much quieter inland, and this may be why so many foreigners have chosen this spot to set up their homes. The church of Sant Joan Baptista is perched at the top of the town of Calvià; it has a beautiful viewing point and is surrounded by old streets lined with imposing mansions and heritage landmarks such as the rainwater cisterns. On the outskirts, among pine forests there are paths that are popular with hikers who are attracted by the bewitching mountain of Es Galatzó.

Ses Illetes

A charming spot which takes its name from the three islets, or *illetes*, of Sa Caleta, Sa Torre and S'Estenedor which make its coastline particularly distinctive. It was one of Mallorca's first tourist resorts and became a favourite honeymoon destination for many couples from the mainland from the 1950s onwards. Its coastline consists of two small coves with sandy beaches, Sa Caleta and Cala Comtessa, where celebrities, including the actors Errol Flynn, Tyrone Power and Rita Hayworth, used to swim. Although crowded in high season, a lot of people live in Illetes throughout the year due to its proximity to the sea and the wide range of services and facilities it offers.

Palmanova

One of Calvià's largest resorts named after one of the first purpose-built tourist complexes on Mallorca. It was designed in 1934, but building work was interrupted by the Spanish Civil War and didn't resume until the 1970s. It has three sandy beaches: Es Carregador, Palmanova and Son Maties, bordered by a long promenade dotted with pavement cafés and restaurants serving local and international cuisine.

The peak of Es Galatzó

Ses Illetes

Palmanova

It is also steeped in history: in 1229, the Knights of Montcada, who had accompanied King Jaume I on his conquest of Mallorca, were buried here on a site marked by a cross.

Magaluf

Magaluf is located between Sa Porrassa point and Cala Vinyes and is particularly popular with foreigners, especially young tourists from the UK. It began to expand as a resort in the 1960s and today it offers a plethora of hotels, bars, discotheques and shopping malls, a water park and countless other attractions. Its beach is 1,600 m long and overlooks the islet of Sa Porrassa. Some historians believe that the name Magaluf is Arabic in origin and comes from the words *ma haluf*, meaning "dirty water", a reference to the stagnant water which was found there in years gone by.

Magaluf beach

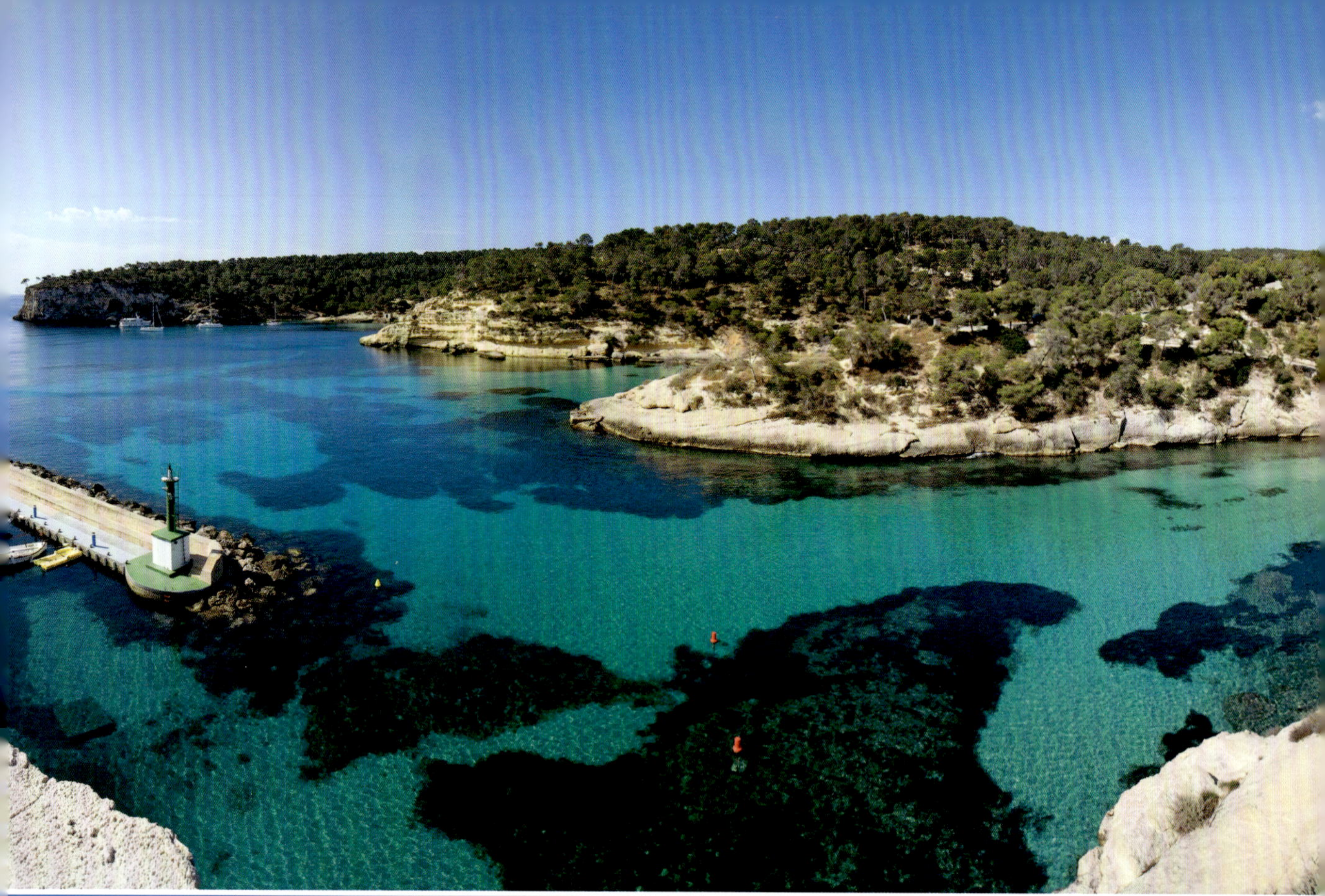
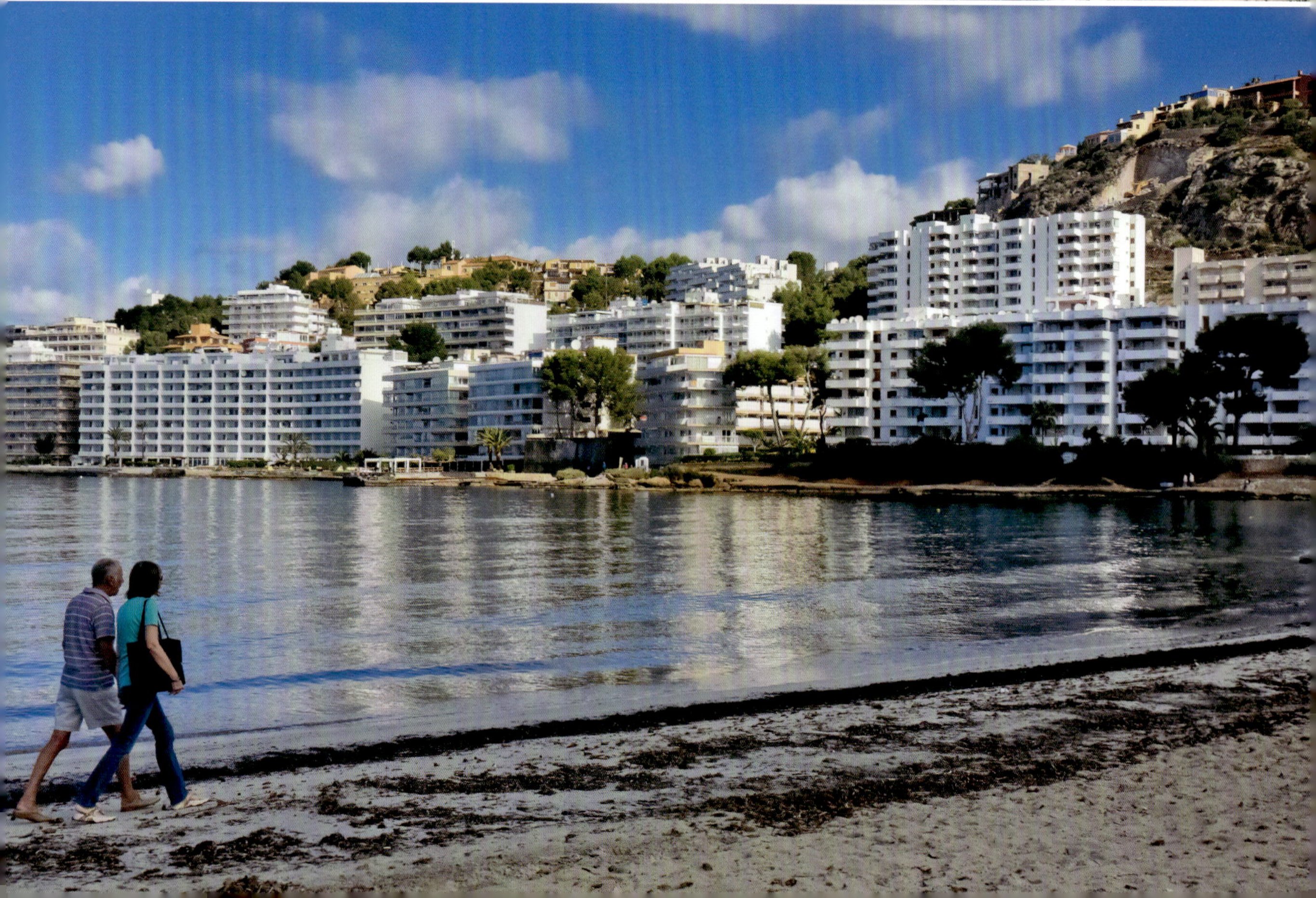

The Bay of Palma

Portals Vells

Portals Vells is a sandy beach at the western tip of the Bay of Palma. It never gets crowded and is popular with families. One of its coves was the first official nudist beach in Calvià. It is known as El Mago, because, in 1967, it was the location for the film *The Magus*, starring Michael Caine, Anthony Quinn, Candice Bergen and Anna Karina. The beach is surrounded by a golf course and a pine forest. On one of its banks you can still see the old quarries where the sandstone to build the cathedral was extracted. The locals nicknamed them *portals* (doorways), because of their resemblance to a large doorway, hence the current name of the beach.

Santa Ponça

Families from around the world flock to this major tourist resort in summer. Curiously enough, it is the favourite destination of Irish visitors, followed by the Scots, Dutch and Italians. Many foreigners made their homes in Santa Ponça, drawn to the beach with its crystal-clear waters and many amenities. It is also a place steeped in history. The troops that seized Mallorca from the Arabs landed here on 10th September 1229. This event is commemorated every year during the local festival, the *Festes del Rei En Jaume* which stages a mock battle between Moors and Christians on the beach. The landing is marked by a stone cross known as the *Creu del Desembarcament*.

Portals Vells

Malgrats Islands

↖ Portals Vells
← Santa Ponça

Ponent

Coast of Andratx with Sa Dragonera in the background

Ponent

The towns of Andratx, Estellencs and Banyalbufar overlook the sea and the mountain range known as the Serra de Tramuntana. Tourist hubs, such as Port d'Andratx, Camp de Mar and Sant Elm have been built around its beautiful beaches, along with smaller, more unspoilt resorts that are tucked away and more popular with families such as Cala Estellencs and Cala Banyalbufar. In the hills, countless paths wind their way around the alluring peak, Puig de Galatzó, which is steeped in legend. One of Mallorca's most unique natural sites stands off the coast of Andratx: the Parc Natural de Sa Dragonera, an island in the shape of a sleeping dragon inhabited by lizards and seabirds.

Andratx

With more than 8,000 inhabitants, Andratx is a peaceful town which is a hive of activity every Wednesday when the weekly market is held. One of the local landmarks is Son Mas, a property dating back to the 15th century and which is now the town hall. It has elegant stone steps and has been renovated several times. The district of Es Pantaleu makes up the old town and is the site of the windmills of Sa Planeta and the tower, the Torre de So Na Gaiana.

Port d'Andratx

Once a small fishing village, this wide natural port, with its crystal-clear waters, is dotted with coves, such as Cala Llamp, Cala Moragues and Cala d'Egos. It is now a magnet for high-end tourism, with much of its coastline developed and built up within an inch of its life. The old defence towers, such as Sant Carles, with Sa Dragonera on the horizon, are still standing. They were built to alert the villagers to pirate attacks. At night, the waterfront is buzzing with activity.

Es Camp de Mar

This tiny resort overlooks a long strip of sand bathed by shimmering, crystal-clear waters. It experienced a boom in the 1980s, although the first tourist establishment, the Gran Hotel, was built in 1932. The islet of S'Illeta faces the beach and is attached to the land by a wooden walkway.

Sant Elm

This is where the troops of Jaume I dropped anchor before landing at Santa Ponça in 1229. Until the early 20th century, Sant Elm made a living from fishing and salt fish, but today it is a peaceful holiday destination with superb views of Sa Dragonera. There are hotels and summer holiday homes around the sandy beaches of Sa Gran and Sa Petita. On a high piece of land stands La Trapa where a community of Franciscan monks built a monastery around 1810.

Andratx Town Hall

Port d'Andratx

↑ Es Camp de Mar   ↓ Sant Elm

Parc Natural de
Sa Dragonera

This important natural park protects the islets of Pantaleu and Mitjana and the island of Sa Dragonera. It covers 274 ha of land which have been declared a Site of Community Importance and a Special Protection Area for birds. Sa Dragonera stands off the coast of Andratx, and is separated from dry land by a channel of water, which is 18 m wide and up to 15 m deep. The island is synonymous with the local ecology movement, which launched a vigorous campaign against attempts to develop the site in the 1970s.

The park is small and its geographical features make it particularly rich in flora and fauna: 361 plant species have been identified, 18 of them endemic to the Balearic Islands. The most widespread plant community is the wild olive tree which grows on scrubland, while the sea beds are covered in meadows of *Posidonia oceanica*, or Neptune grass, which provide refuge for countless underwater species.

The fauna includes a lizard population made up of an endemic subspecies that is found nowhere else in the world. The birds are the noisiest inhabitants, with species such as Audouin's gull (*Larus audouinii*), the Balearic shearwater (*Puffinus mauretanicus*) —which is native to the islands— and the largest population of Eleanora's falcon (*Falco eleonorae*) on the Balearic Islands. At night, the bats come out. Up to five species have been identified so far.

Sa Dragonera

Parc Natural de Sa Dragonera **Ponent** 41

Estellencs

This town, with its rich heritage and wealth of flora and fauna, has known how to preserve its identity, far from the effects of mass tourism, and retains some of its traditional means of subsistence, such as farming. In the old town, you can still see the medieval legacy in the narrow cobbled streets lined with stone houses. The church of Sant Joan Baptista (17th c.) has a defence tower crowned by a bell tower. There are also remains of the ancient water-distribution system devised by the Arabs, which includes laundry troughs, water tanks, cisterns and ancient water channels.

Es Galatzó

Standing 1,027 m high, the Puig de Galatzó is one of the most impressive mountains on the Serra de Tramuntana, and falls within the boundaries of Calvià, Estellencs and Puigpunyent. It is steeped in symbolism and is the highest point on the west side of the island. Legends about the mountain abound, such as those concerning Es Comte Mal, the second Count of Santa Maria de Formiguera. A nobleman, who lived in the 17th century, he was involved in a number of legal wrangles and spread terror throughout the area. Due to his extreme cruelty, he was condemned to ride for eternity on his horse surrounded by flames. The top of Galatzó boasts views of almost all the island.

Cala Estellencs

Locals and summer holidaymakers from Estellencs usually sunbathe and swim on this rocky beach bathed by crystal-clear waters and surrounded by sheer, reddish-coloured rocks. On the right, there is a small landing stage with the typical huts, known as *escars*, where the fishermen would keep their traditional sailing boats, or *llaüts*, which are now motor-powered. The beach is practically unspoilt and forms a peaceful landscape. As you look at it, it's hard to believe that, in days gone by, it was subject to attacks, as the defence towers along the coast testify. They were part of the system designed to warn the islanders that pirate ships were approaching.

Estellencs

↑ Es Galatzó   ↓ Cala Estellencs

Banyalbufar

A peaceful village on the western coast of the island set on a steep hillside. It overlooks the sea and has terraced hillsides dating back hundreds of years. Today they are planted with Malvasia vines, a grape variety typical to the area, and the *tomàtiga de ramellet*, a local variety of tomato grown on the vine which is an essential ingredient to make a delicious *pa amb oli*, or bread rubbed with tomato and drizzled with olive oil. The terraces are irrigated by a system dating from Islamic times which includes irrigation ditches, channels and fountains. One of the main landmarks is Sa Baronia, a 16th-century mansion with a beautiful interior courtyard, or *clastra*.

Banyalbufar sands

Stepped street in Banyalbufar

Banyalbufar **Ponent** 45

Es Verger tower

Torre des Verger
This watchtower, which is also known as the Torre de Ses Ànimes, is steeped in legends about ghostly apparitions. Perched on the cliffs above the Banyalbufar coast, in days gone by it communicated with other similar towers using smoke signals during the day and fire at night.

Cala Banyalbufar
A beautiful, rocky cove which is practically unspoilt except for a series of fishermen's huts which actually make it more beautiful. A freshwater stream flows down the cliffs like a waterfall into the limpid waters where locals from Banyalbufar go to swim.

Port des Canonge
One of the most charming and genuine spots on the western coast of Mallorca, with its shingle beaches where Neptune grass washes up in winter. The cove provides a tiny harbour on this steep stretch of the coast which offers little shelter to boats. Bathed by crystal-clear waters, the beach is surrounded by the typical fishermen's huts, or *escars*, where small boats are still stored to protect them from the harsh storms. You can also see the wooden rails that are used to take the boats, or *llaüts*, down to the sea.

Cala Banyalbufar

Port des Canonge

Tramuntana

Sa Foradada

Tramuntana

The Serra de Tramuntana is a mountain range that forms the backbone of the north-west of the island. In 2011 it was awarded World Heritage status by UNESCO in the Cultural Landscape category in recognition of the symbiosis between human beings and nature throughout the centuries, on land where culture, legends, traditions, spirituality and identity merge. Travellers and artists of every epoch, such as George Sand, Frédéric Chopin and Robert Graves, have stopped off at its villages over the centuries and found them a source of inspiration. Hikers from all over the world have explored the hundreds of paths that criss-cross this mountain range and are part of the GR-211, the *Ruta de la Pedra en Sec*, or drystone wall route.

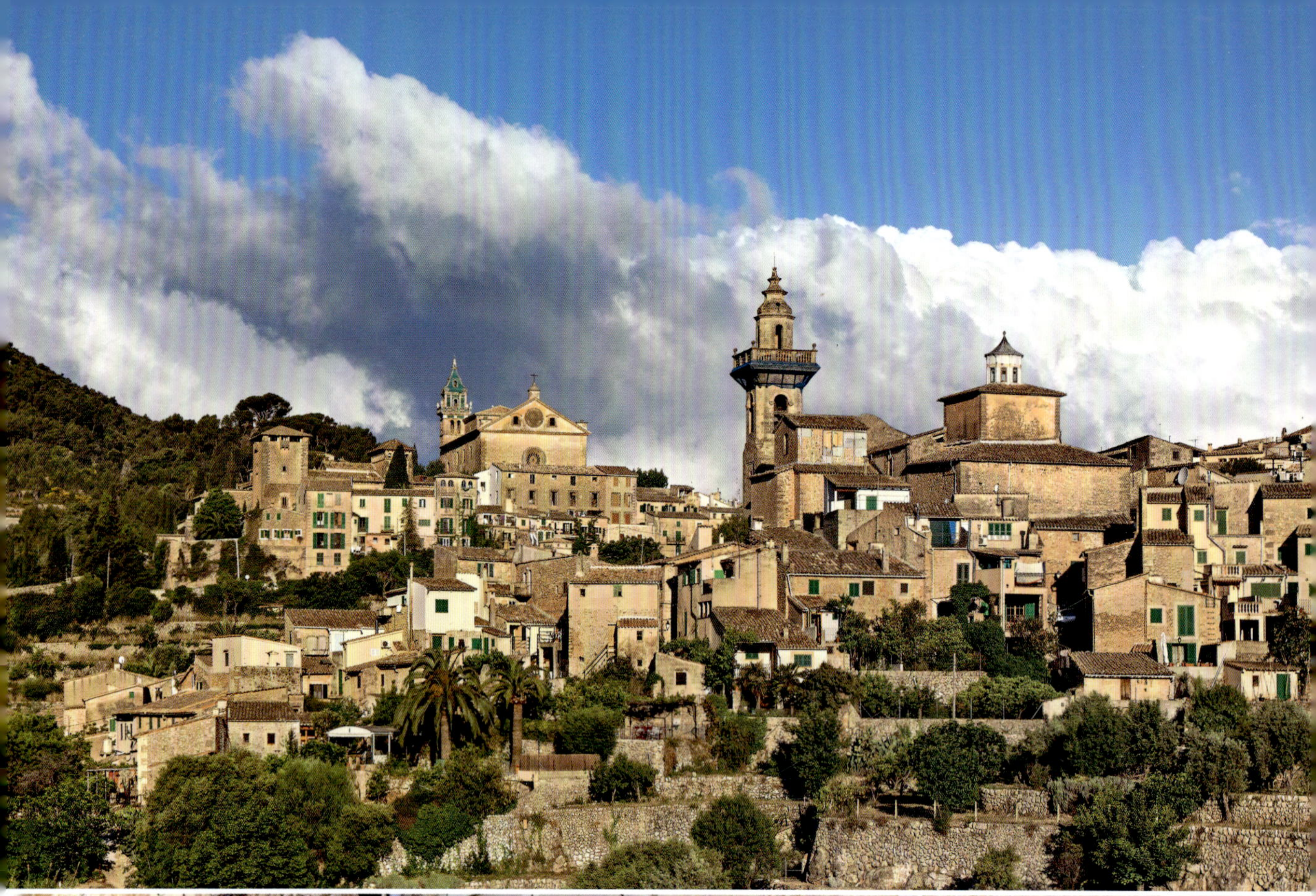

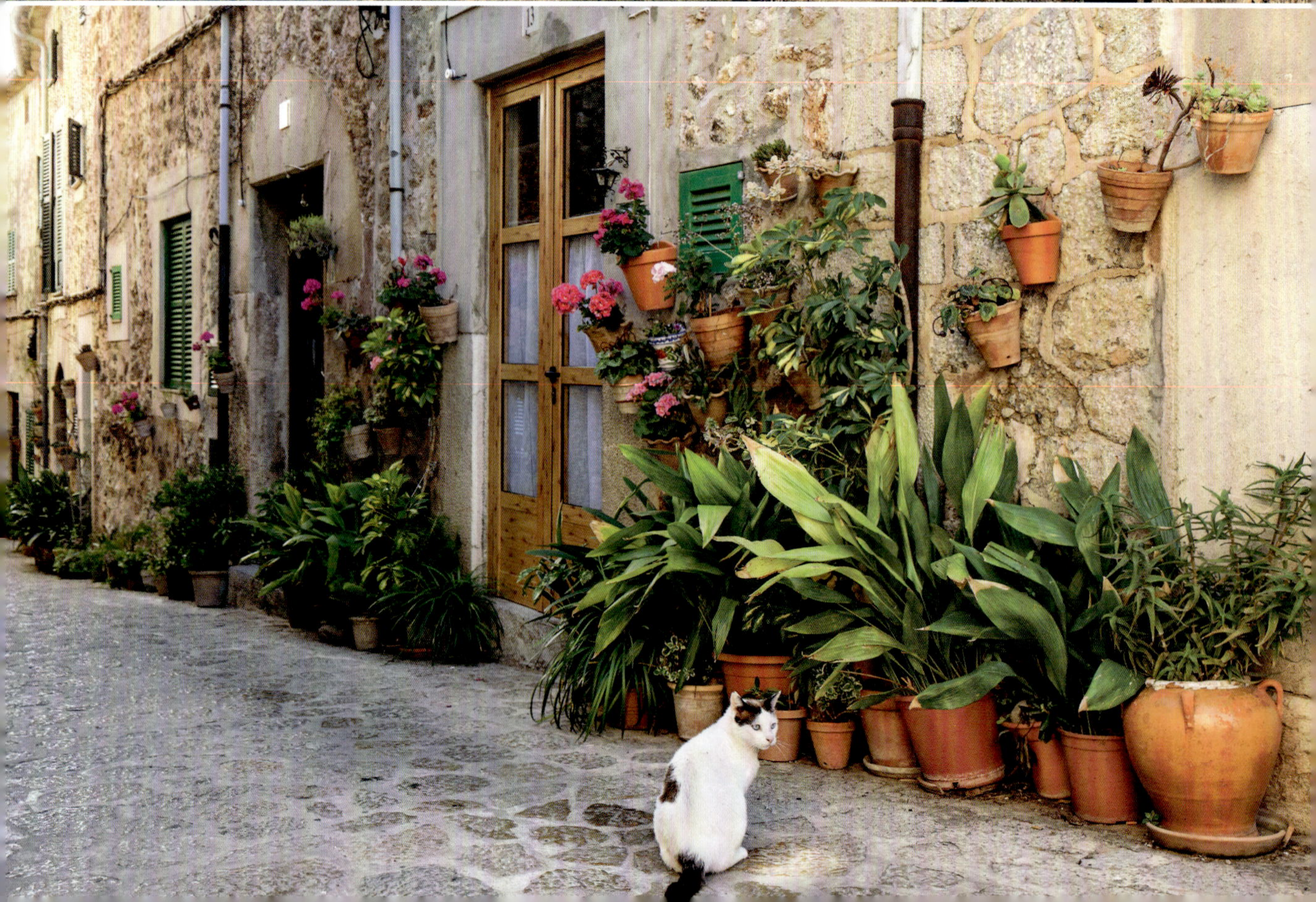

Valldemossa

Nestling among valleys and surrounded by lush countryside, this picturesque village also has an abundance of fountains and allotments. Some of the stone houses on its steep, narrow streets, decorated with plant pots, feature the religious symbol of Mallorca's patron saint, Catalina Tomàs, who was born in 1531. The village has attracted travellers and artists throughout the centuries, including the painter and writer Santiago Rusiñol and Archduke Ludwig Salvator of Austria.

La Cartoixa
Imposing building overlooking the Valldemossa landscape which bears witness to much of its local history. The monastery was originally the residence of the kings of Mallorca and Carthusian monks lived here between 1399 and 1835. It has a valuable art collection.

Chopin's cell
One of the cells inside La Cartoixa where Chopin worked. It houses the Pleyel piano which the musician used to finish his *Preludes* and to work on compositions including the second *Ballad No. 2 in F Major, op. 38*.

Port de Valldemossa
A winding road emerges into this tiny fishing port with its crystal-clear waters. It is now a peaceful summer-holiday spot with restaurants where you can sample excellent freshly caught fish.

La Cartoixa

Bust of Chopin

Port de Valldemossa

Miramar

Miramar was a monastery built in 1276 by Ramon Llull to teach Franciscan monks Arabic so that they would be able to persuade the Moors to convert to Christianity on their travels through North Africa. The property went through a number of owners until it was purchased by Archduke Ludwig Salvator of Austria in 1872, a nobleman who had fallen in love with Mallorca. He restored and transformed it adding artistic elements from Italy, France and Bohemia. The building still has four columns from Llull's Gothic monastery, and the chapel has an image of the Virgin made from Carrara marble, a gift from the Empress Elisabeth of Austria who visited the archduke during the winters of 1892 and 1893.

Sa Foradada

An imposing promontory in the characteristic stone of the northern coast with an 18 m hole in the centre. In 1582 it bore witness to the battle in which 150 corsairs from North Africa were defeated by some 50 islanders on the orders of Mateu Sanglada. A path which begins in Son Marroig leads to Sa Foradada.

S'Estaca

A tiny village with simple stone houses right by the sea. Popular with summer visitors who are lucky enough to find a place to rent and go there in search of peace and quiet along this stretch of the northern coast. Nearby, stands S'Estaca, one of the properties owned by Archduke Ludwig Salvator of Austria, which drew inspiration from houses in Lipari in Italy.

Son Marroig

This is another of the houses that belonged to Archduke Ludwig Salvator of Austria, who was so enamoured with this stretch of the coastline that he purchased several properties there in the 19th century. Today the house has been turned into a shrine to his memory, with personal mementoes, photos and books and a museum. The small rotunda in the garden boasts the finest views of the northern coast.

Miramar Monastery

S'Estaca

Sa Foradada ↗
Rotunda at Son Marroig →

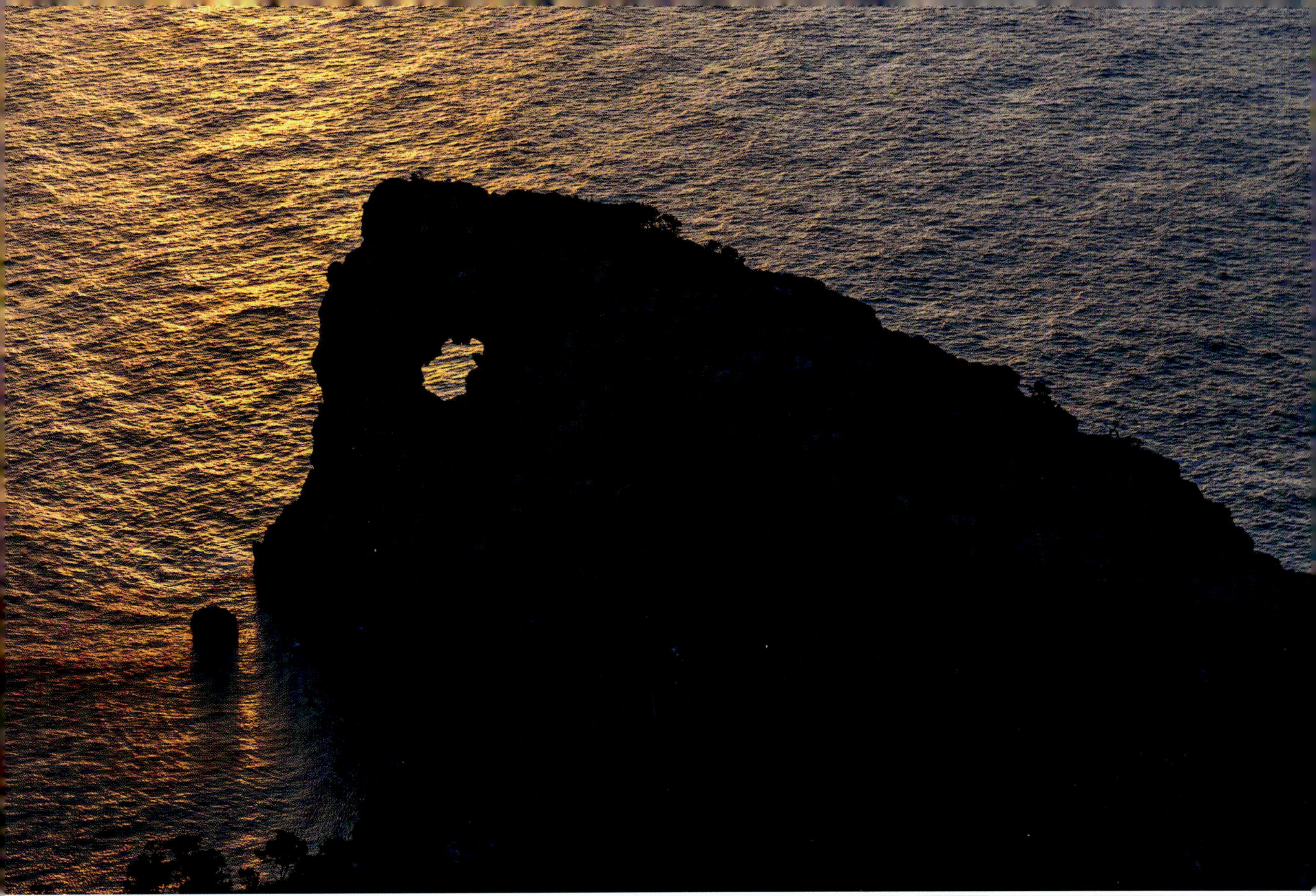

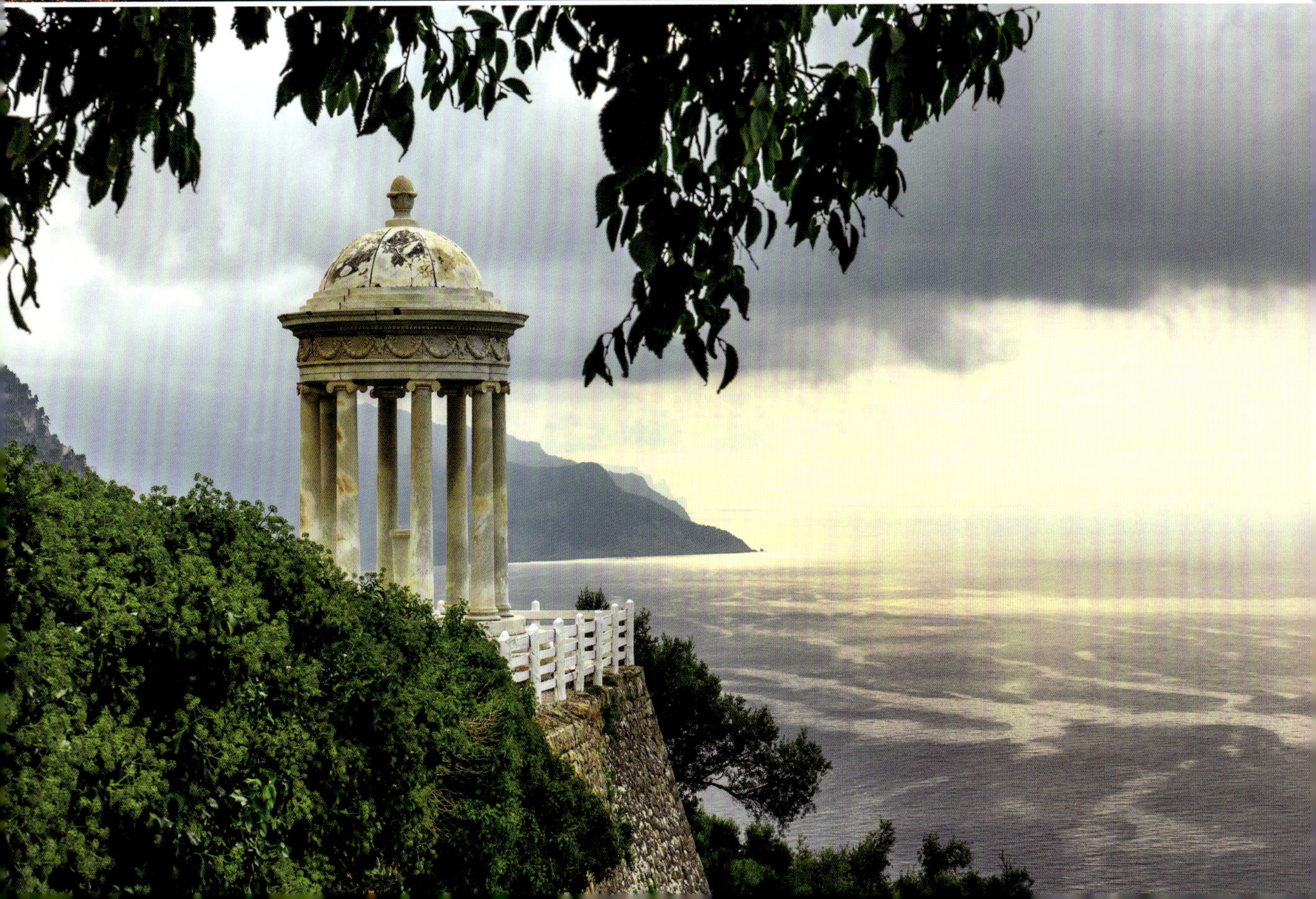

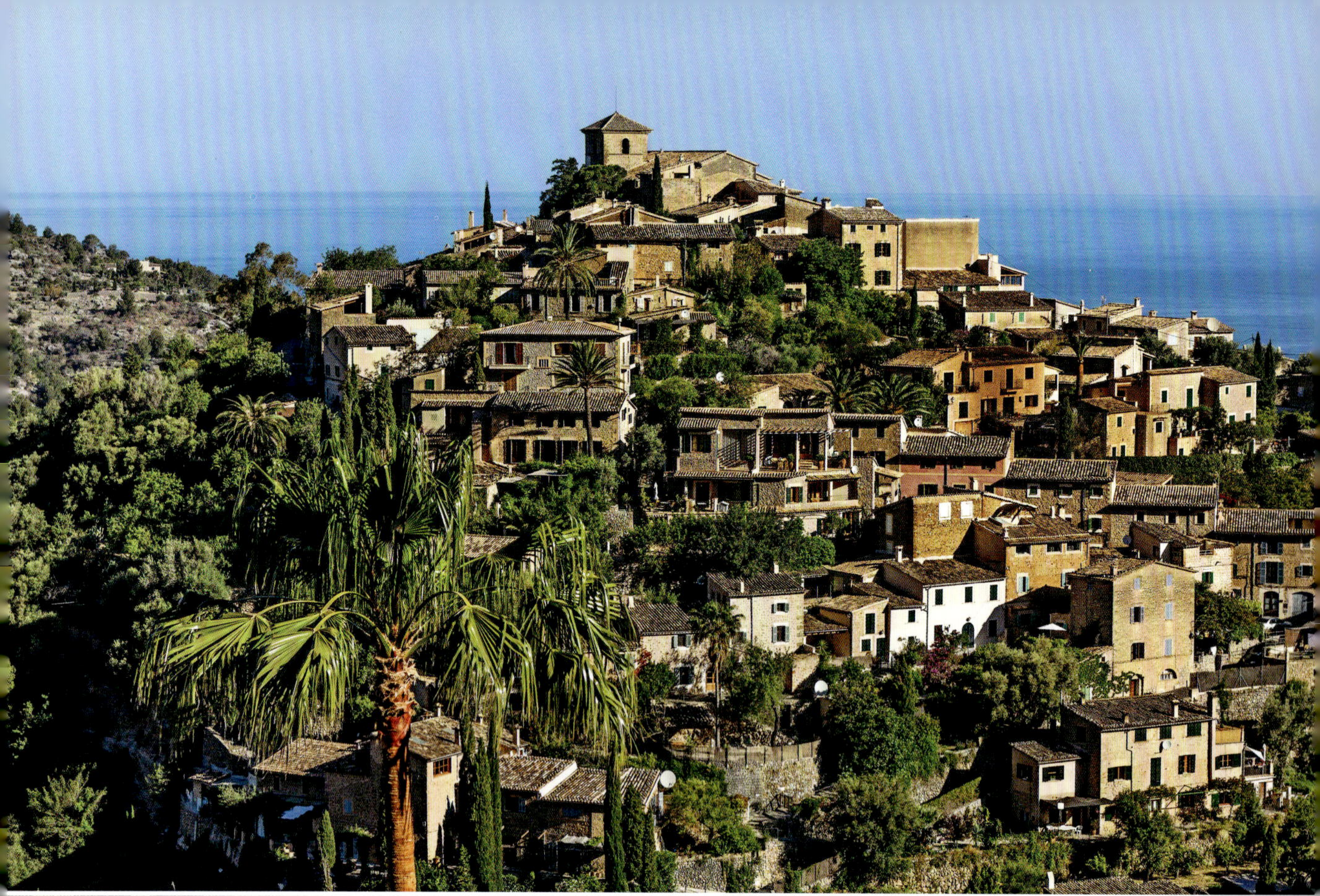

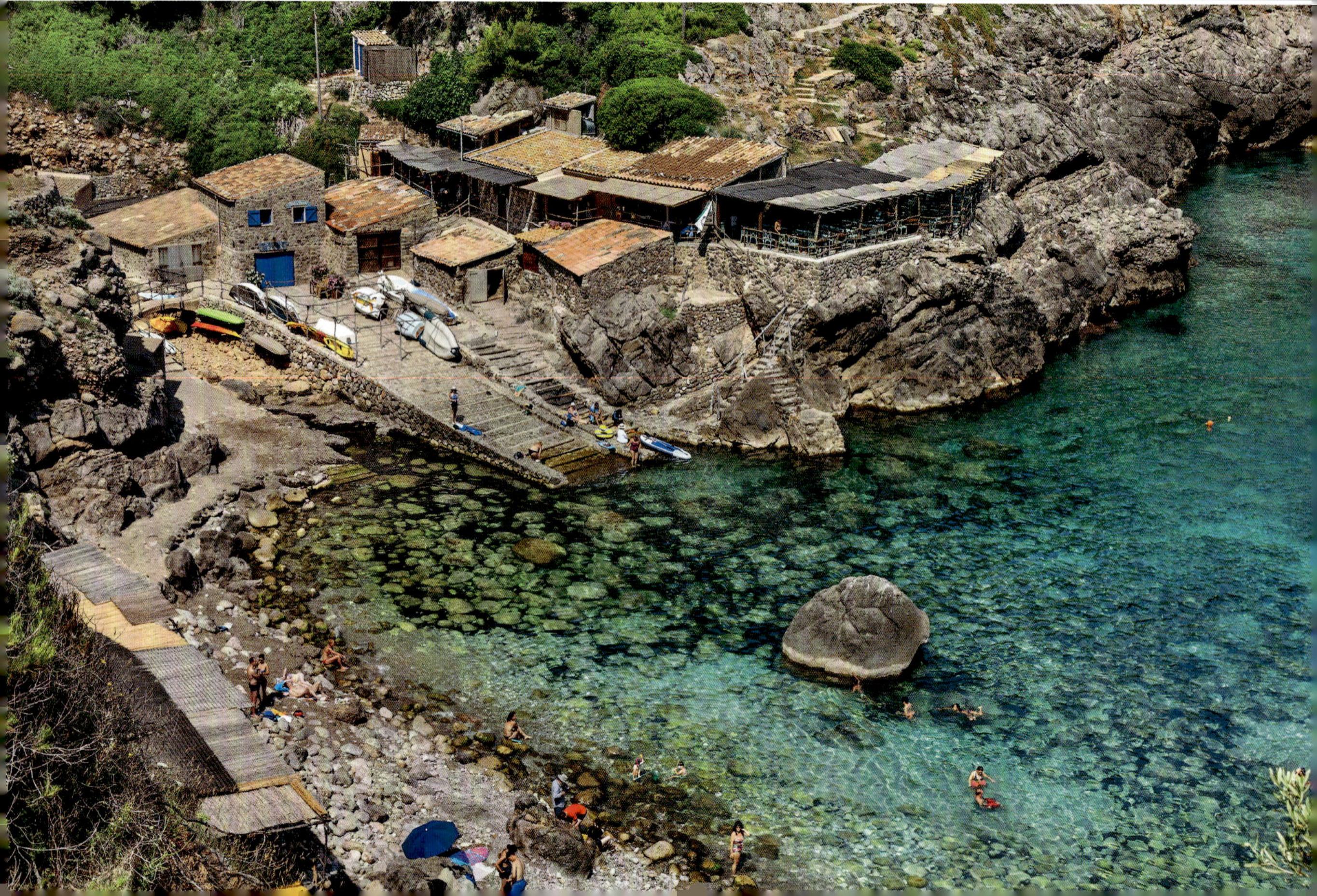

Deià

The artist Santiago Rusiñol described Deià as a fairy-tale village. Set among olive trees and in the shadow of the imposing summit of Mount Teix (1,064 m), in years gone by, the villagers made a living from olive oil, citrus fruit and wool. Pigs were reared and lime and charcoal were produced in the holm oak forests, and snow was gathered from the nearby peaks. From the late 19th century onwards, the landscape captivated artists and bohemians, including Archduke Ludwig Salvator of Austria, the composer Manuel de Falla and the poet Robert Graves, who decided to make Deià his permanent home. At the highest point in the village is one of the most beautiful cemeteries in the Mediterranean.

Cala Deià

This beautiful cove nestles between two small headlands, the Punta de Deià and Punta Son Beltran. It still retains the typical fisherman's huts, known as *escars*, and is a very popular bathing haunt with locals where you'll also see famous faces in summer. The stream, the Torrent Major, flows into the sea and until the middle of the last century vegetables were grown on its slopes.

Llucalcari

Perched on a hillside, this pretty hamlet developed around two ancient properties, Can Simó and Can Apol·loni. There are about 20 houses, some of which still have defence towers. The chapel dedicated to Our Lady of the Forsaken was built in 1600.

Deià

Llucalcari

↖ Deià
← Cala Deià

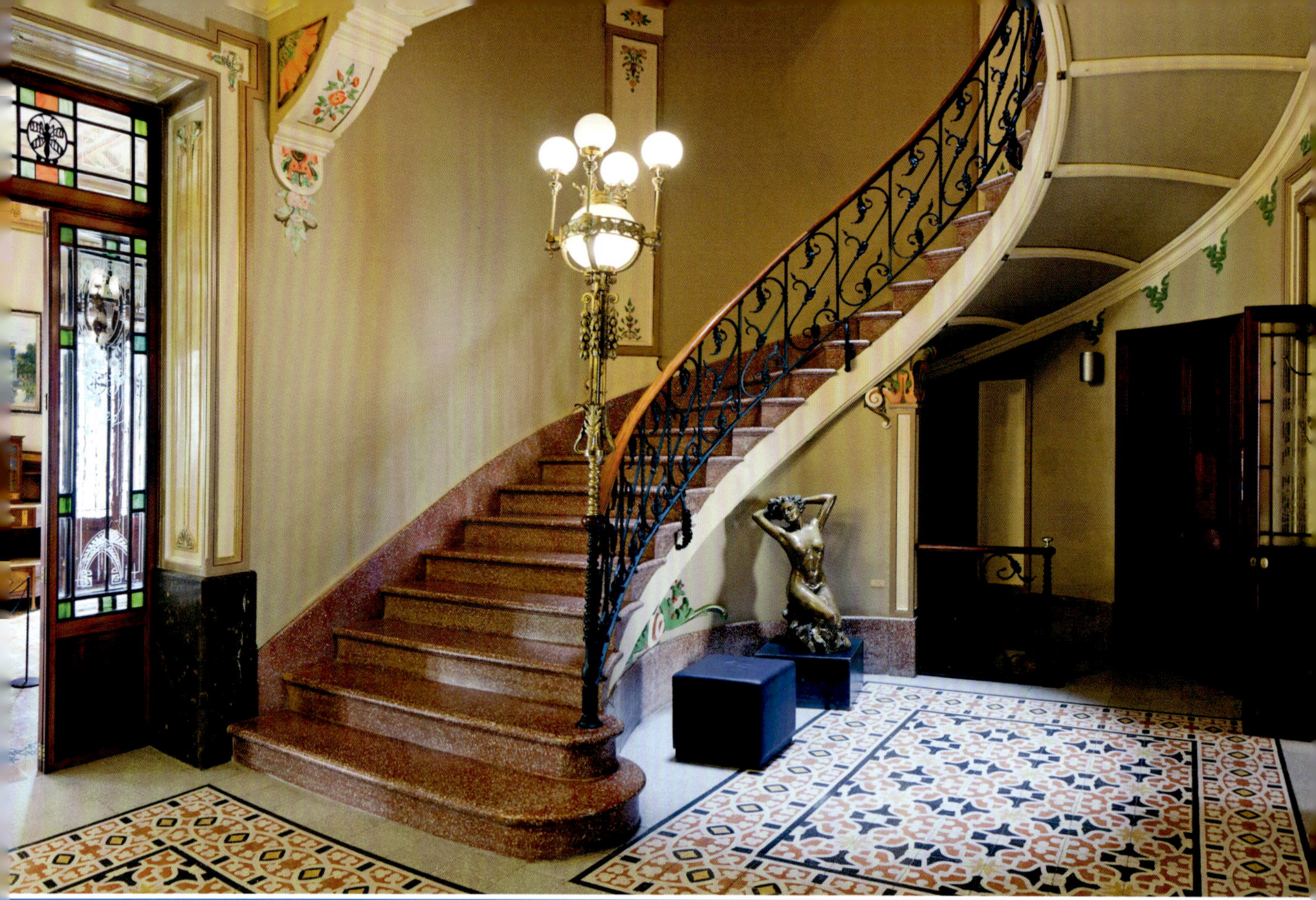

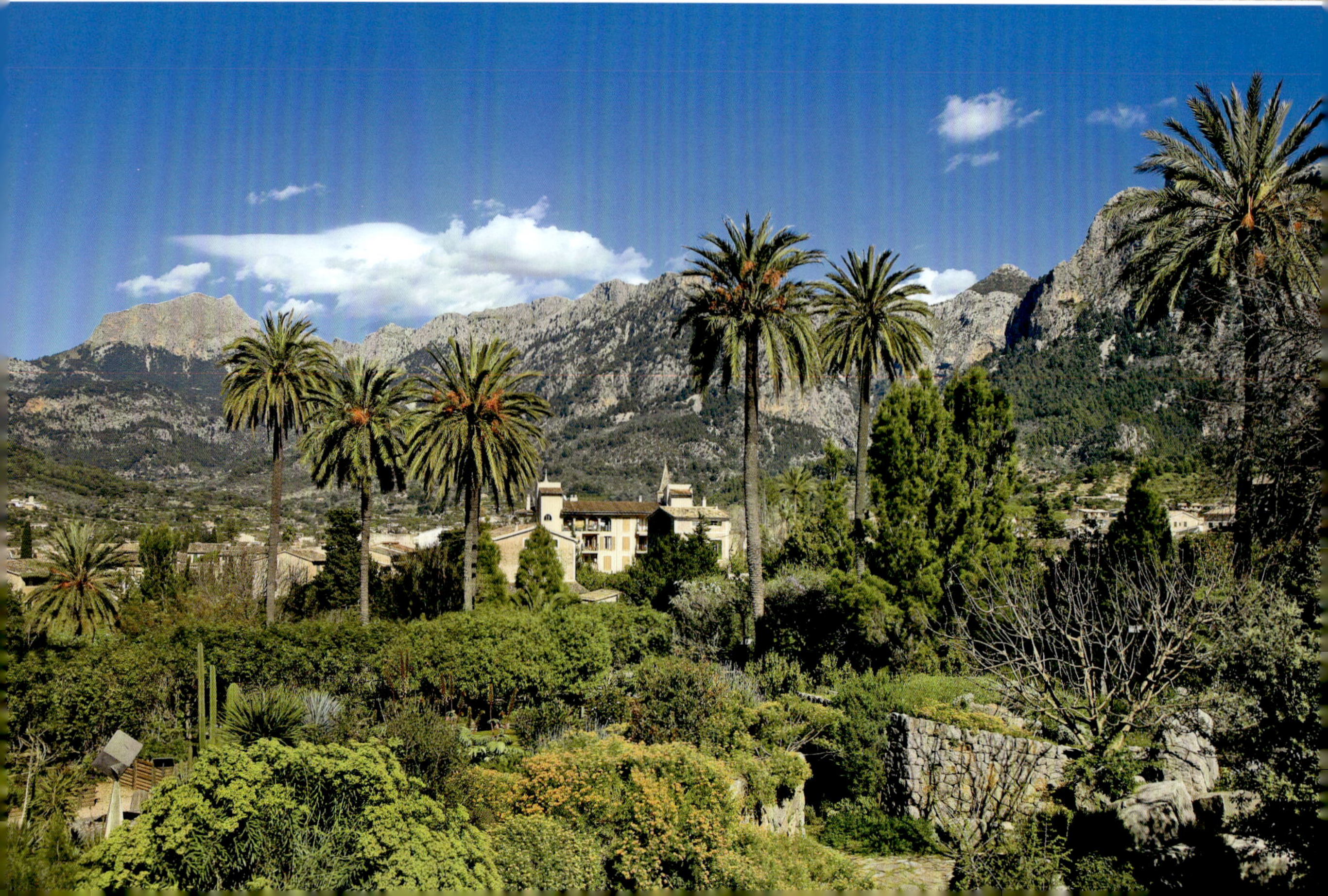

Sóller

Sóller nestles in a fertile mountainous valley which it shares with the village of Fornalutx and the hamlet of Biniaraix. It was awarded town status in 1905 and has numerous bars and shops, where you'll find everything from clothes and local speciality foods to handcrafted goods. The old quarter has cobbled streets lined with elegant houses, some of them evocative of the art-nouveau period. Many of them are mansions built by the locals who had emigrated to France and America in search of work and returned to the island after making their fortunes.

The two main buildings in the central square, the Plaça de la Constitució, are also art-nouveau in style: the church of Sant Bartomeu, designed by the architect Joan Rubió in 1904, and the Banc de Sóller, by the same architect, which was built in 1889 with money from the returning emigrants. The town is also home to the art-nouveau museum, the Museu Modernista de Can Prunera, and the railway station which has a gallery space hosting permanent exhibitions of works by Joan Miró and Pablo Picasso.

A wooden tram operates along the 3 km route between the town and port, a trip that goes through groves of orange trees. When they are in bloom the air is filled with the scent of orange blossom. In May, the town celebrates its local festival commemorates the islanders' defeat of the Saracen invaders in 1561 and includes a mock battle between Moors and Christians which all the locals take part in.

↖ **Can Prunera**
← **Botanical Gardens**

Church of Sant Bartomeu

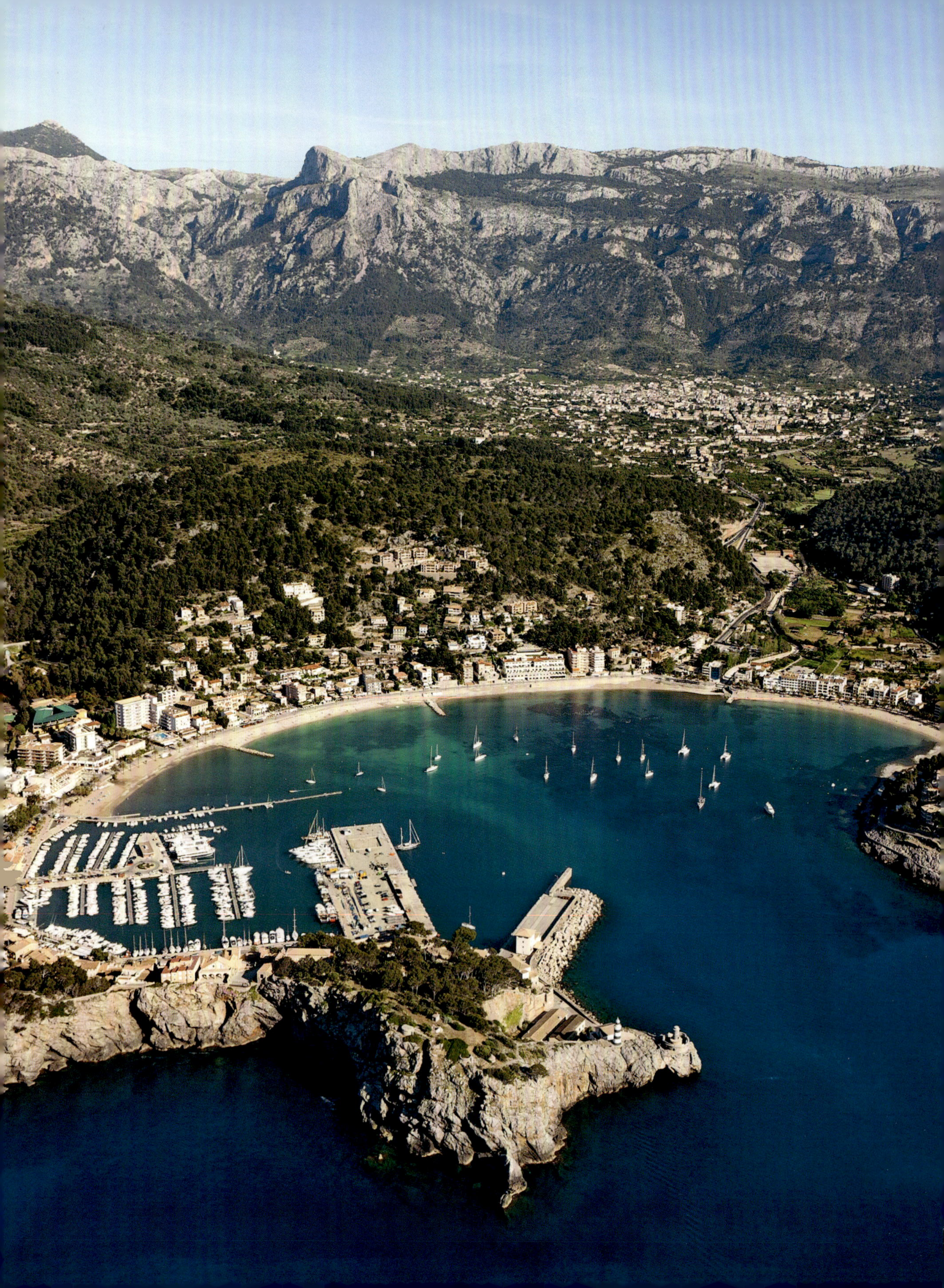

Port de Sóller

This is one of the most sheltered and widest natural harbours on Mallorca. The mouth of the harbour measures 450 m across and further inside expands to 830 m wide. In years gone by, boats laden with oranges, lemons, almonds and olives set sail from the Port de Sóller, most of them bound for France. Many of the islanders married people from France as a result and French is still spoken in some homes and shops. A tourist resort has grown around the harbour, with its modern sports facilities, although it still retains the flavour of an old fishing port with its ancient fisherman's chapel, dedicated to Santa Caterina. The town has two beaches, En Repic and Des Través, which are overlooked by the Torre Picada, and a pleasant seafront promenade which leads to the lighthouse.

Sóller tram

Port de Sóller

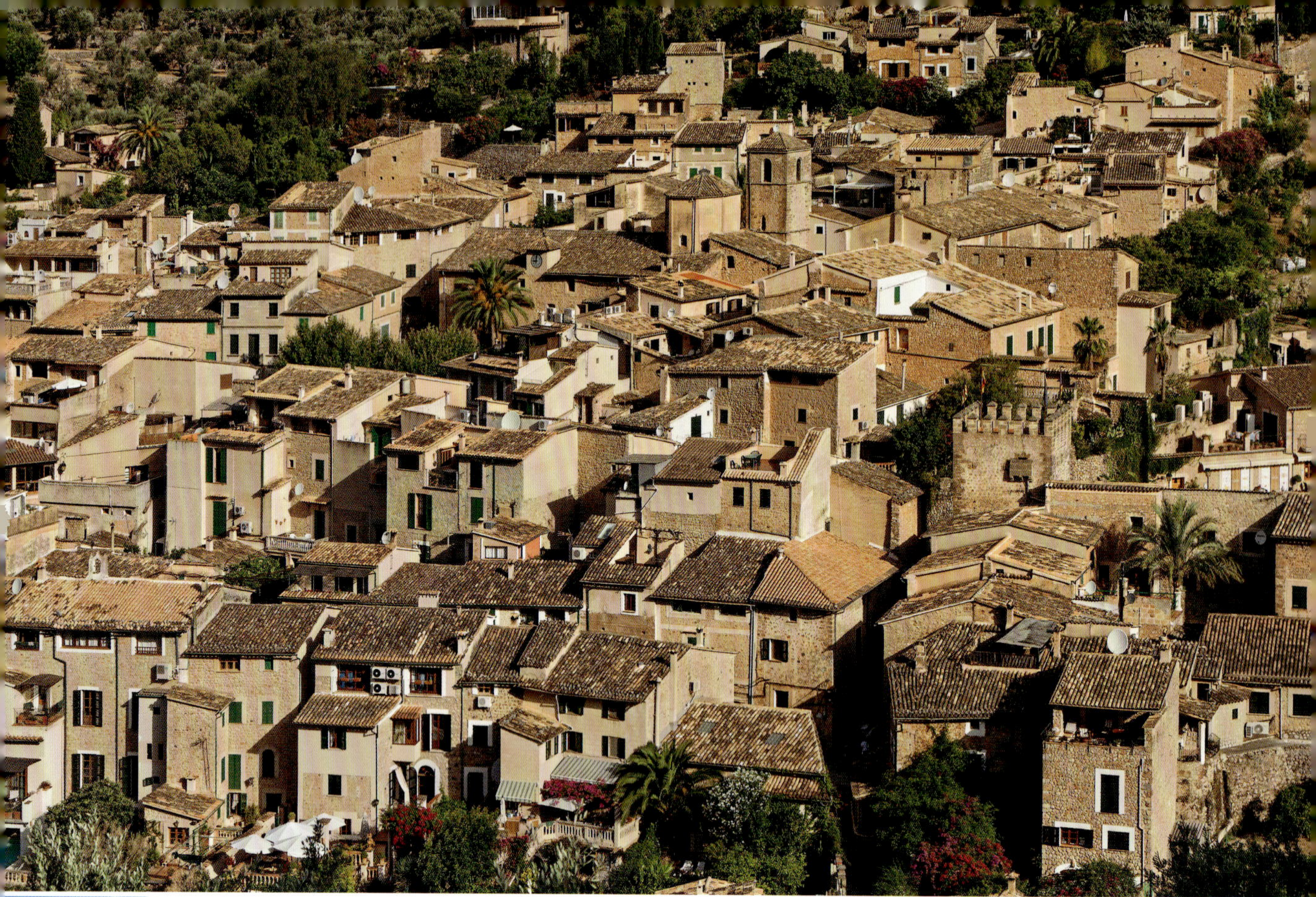

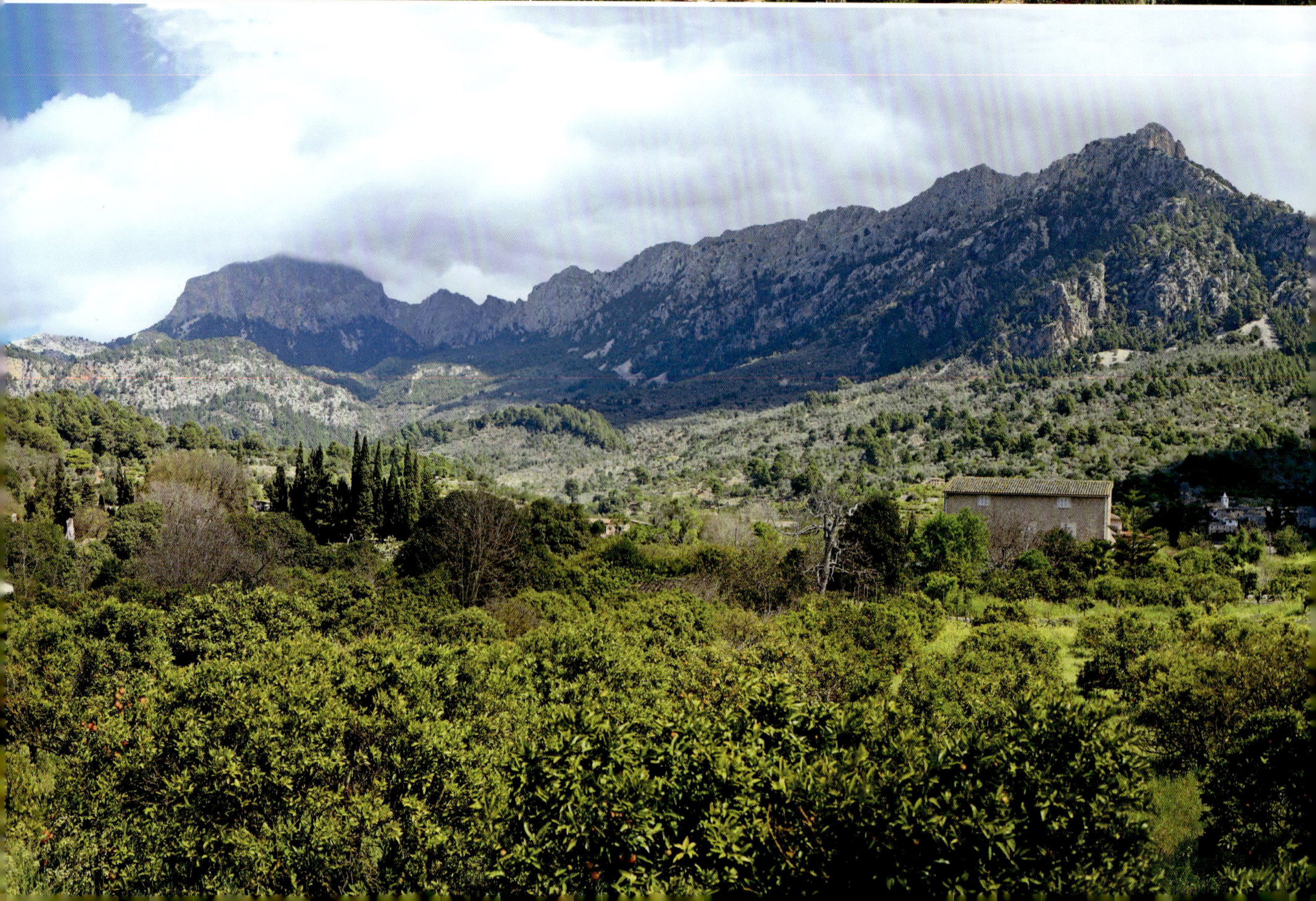

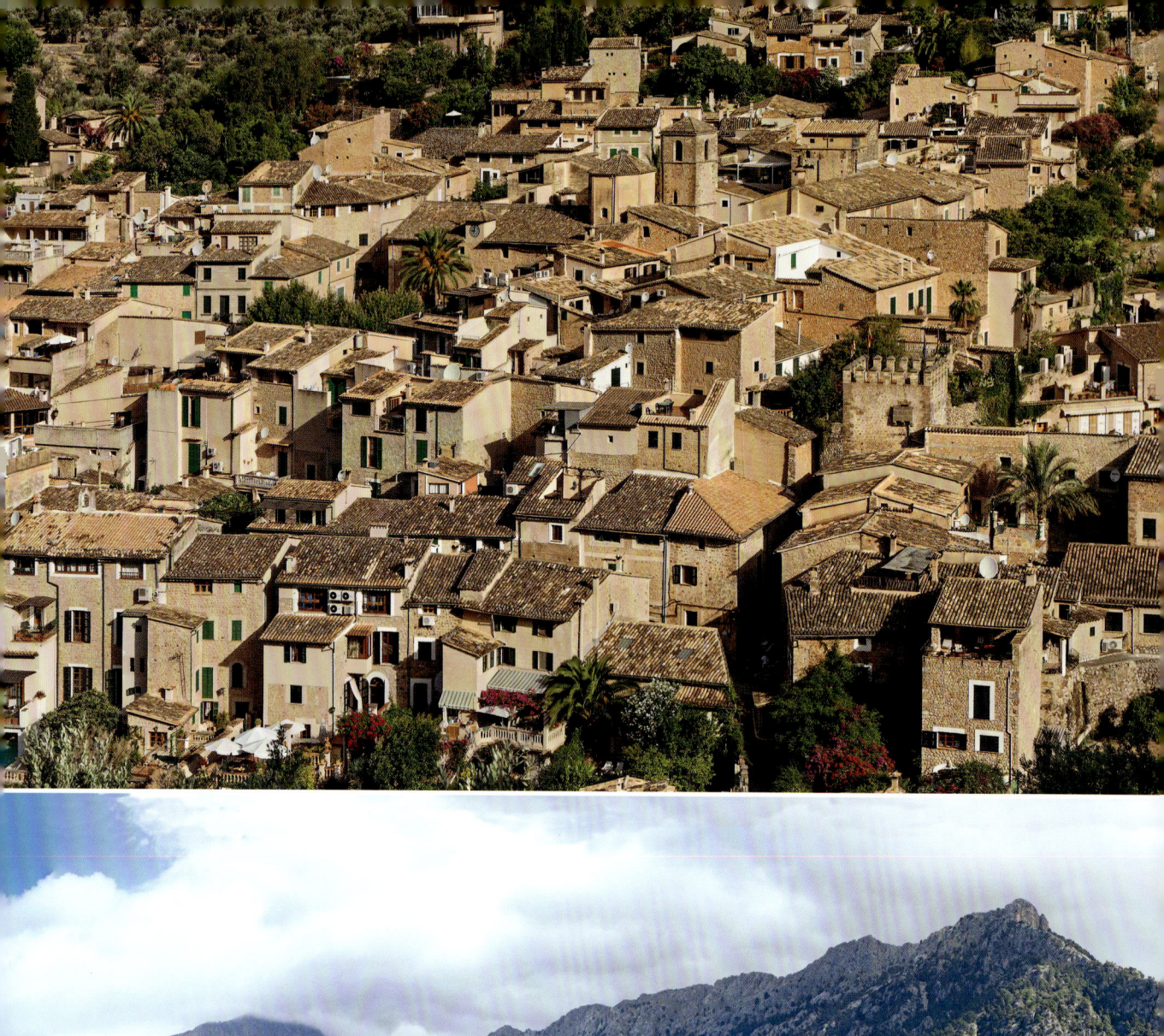

Fornalutx

This mountain village was part of the municipality of Sóller until 1813 meaning that the history of both places is closely entwined. Fornalutx still retains the Arabic layout of narrow, cobbled streets and steps have been incorporated into some of the steeper stretches. More than 30 houses have painted tiles under the eaves. This decorative resource was widespread during the 16th century and the tiles feature an assortment of geometrical, plant and animal motifs or religious themes drawn in red. The tiles were painted on site and had a symbolic as well as decorative value. They were used to protect and defend the house and its occupants from any external attacks.

Biniaraix

This small hamlet stands on the site of an Arabic farmstead, which King Jaume I transferred to the Bishop of Girona following the Christian conquest. With nearly 500 inhabitants, it is situated halfway up the Sóller Valley at the foot of the ravine known as the Barranc de Biniaraix, which has a path that is popular with hikers from around the world. The ravine connects the Sóller Valley with the valleys of L'Ofre and Cúber, the monastery and pilgrimage site, the Santuari de Lluc, the village of Orient and the interior of the island. Its 3.5 kilometres length enables us to appreciate the defining elements of what are known as bridle paths, often cobbled and bordered by dry-stone wall constructions, without mortar. The sides of the paths are divided into small plots mostly planted with olive trees, some of them centuries old.

↖ Fornalutx
← Sóller Valley

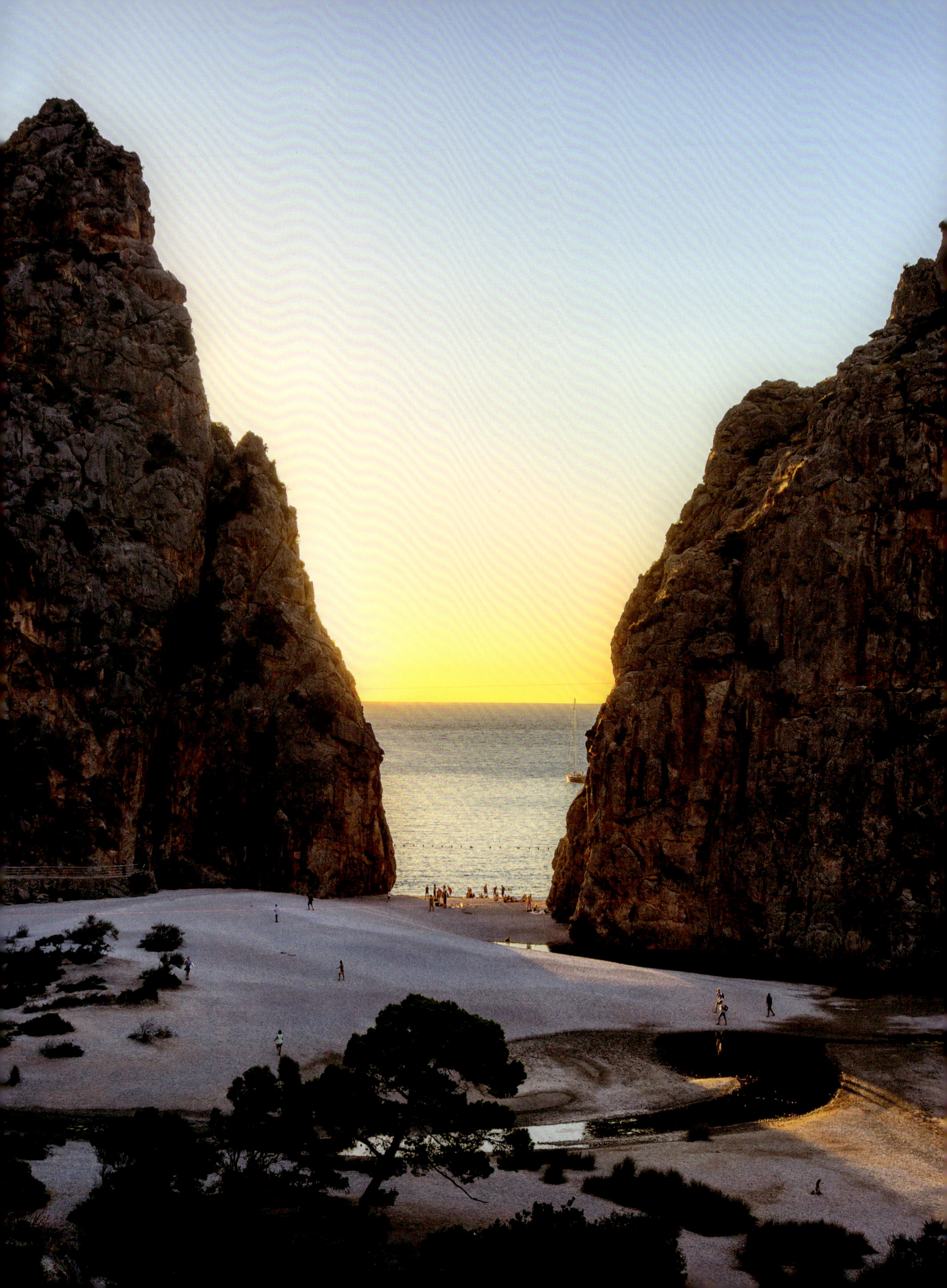

Sa Calobra

Sa Calobra beach, with its boulders and gravel, makes up an imposing landscape at the mouth of the Pareis torrent, an area of outstanding natural beauty which is popular with hikers and canyoners. It nestles between the crags of Morro de sa Vaca and Morro de ses Fel·les, in the shadow of Puig Major (1,445 m), and you can get there by sea —on boats that set sail from Port de Sóller— or by land, along a road running for 14 km that snakes down to the sea from a height of 900 m, with twelve 180° degree bends and one, known as the Nus de sa Corbata, or tie knot, which, as the name suggests, loops back under itself at 360°. A choir concert is held on the beach every year taking advantage of the wonderful natural acoustics.

Torrent de Pareis

The Torrent de Pareis begins at the confluence of the Gorg Blau and Lluc gorges, in an area known as S'Entreforc, and consists of a karstic gorge with walls up to 200 m high. The bed of the gorge descends for almost 3 km until it comes out onto the beautiful Sa Calobra beach. The contours of the gorge are the result of the action of water from torrents on the limestone, which has carved out a peculiar landscape rich in caves and chasms. It is a place of pilgrimage for hikers, potholers and canyoners, as well as biologists because it is home to a small population of Mallorcan midwife toads (*Alytes muletensis*), an amphibian endemic to the Serra de Tramuntana.

Nus de Sa Corbata

Pareis torrent

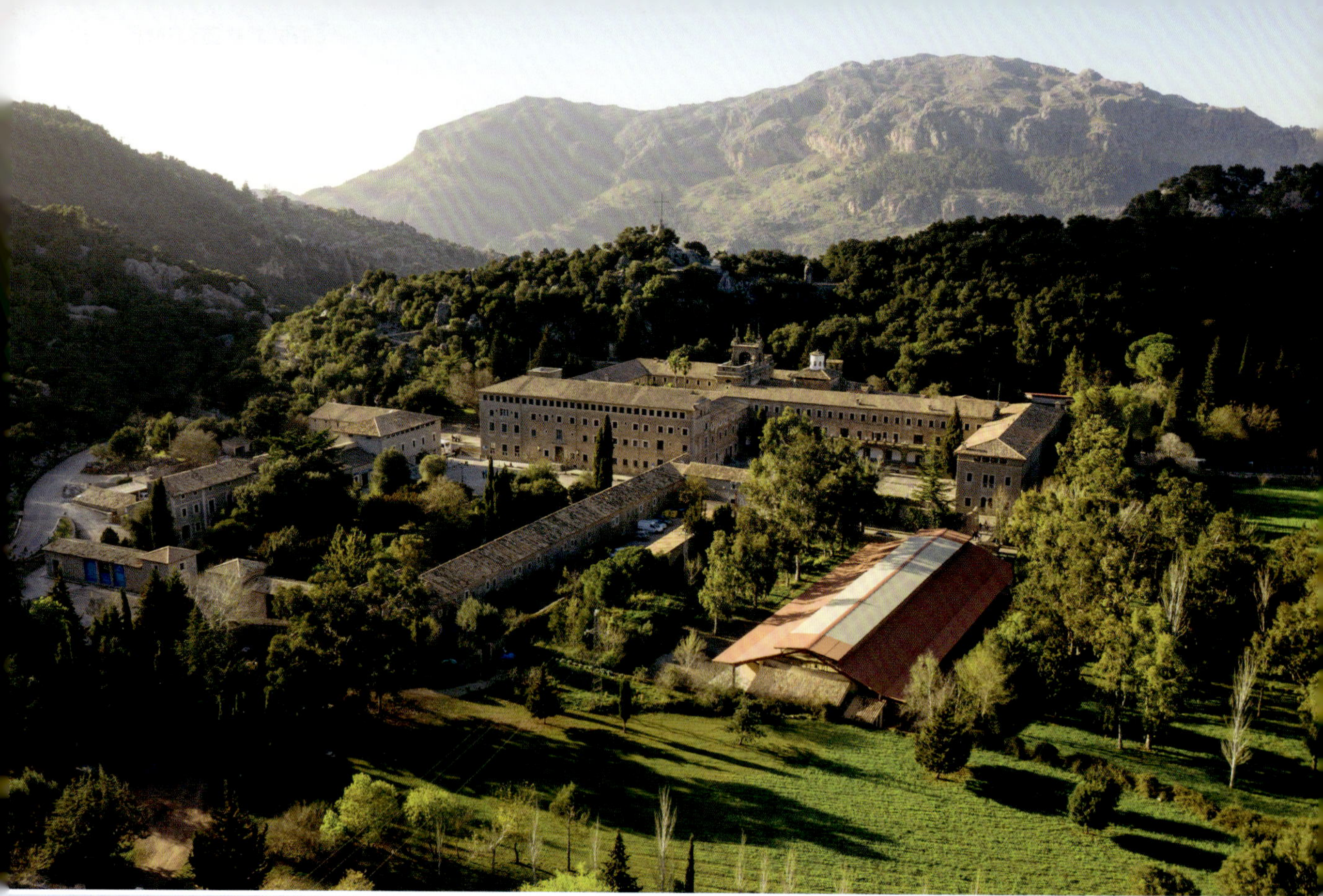

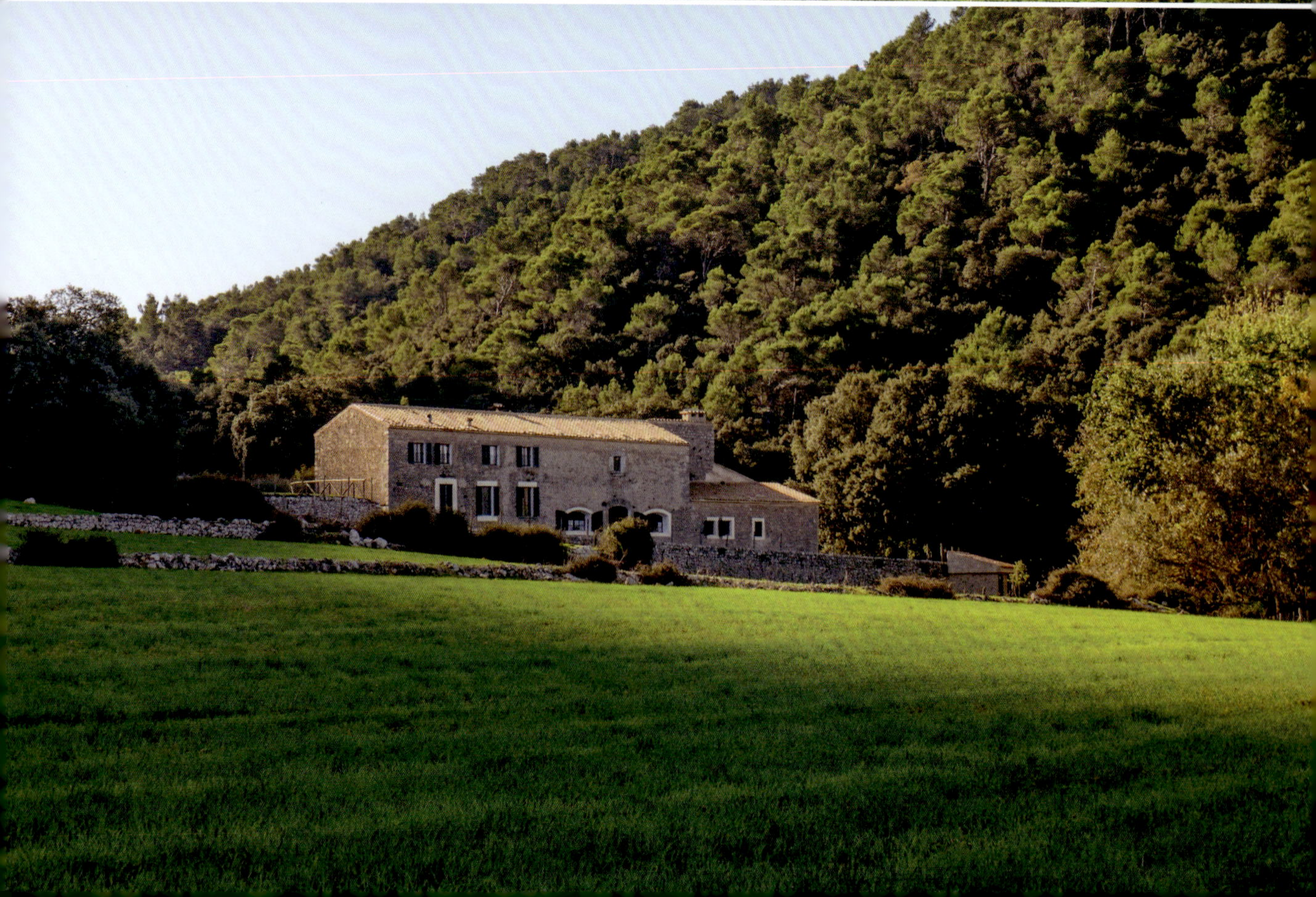

Escorca

Mallorca's largest and least-populated municipality, Escorca is set among the vast holm oak forests in the valley around the Santuari de Lluc and the peaks of Puig Major and Massanella, which are capped with snow in winter. Some of the largest torrents on the island, including Almadrà and Coma Freda, have their sources within the municipal area of Escorca which also includes the communities of Cala Tuent and Sa Calobra. Nestling between the mountains are historic estates such as Mossa, Mortitx and Binifaldó, which were used for years for hunting, and to obtain ice, coal and lime.

Binifaldó

An estate now open to the public with an abundance of water, springs, chasms and holm oaks. It retains elements that bear witness to the centuries-old exploitation of the forest, including lime kilns, charcoal furnaces and drystone walls. There is a shelter on the estate.

Santuari de Lluc

The spiritual heart of Mallorca beats in the forests, mountains and at the Santuari de Lluc. The sanctuary has a hostelry, known as the *Porxets*, which were originally designed as lodgings for pilgrims who visited Lluc and are now available as guest accommodation. The Renaissance-style basilica was built between 1622 and 1691 and has a Latin-cross floor plan, a central nave, and three chapels on each side. There is also statue of a black madonna made of painted sandstone, which dates from the 13th to 14th centuries.

The Lluc Valley

An absolute must for hikers and walkers who can make their way up the highest peaks on the island, such as Puig de Massanella, Tomir, Puig d'en Galileu and Puig Roig. There is an abundance of caves, torrents and old pilgrims' paths that link up to villages such as Inca and Pollença.

Santuari de Lluc

Porches or *porxets* of Lluc

← Lluc Valley
← Public estate of Binifaldó

Paratge Natural de la
Serra de Tramuntana

The Serra de Tramuntana forms the backbone of the north-west of the island. Covering a distance of 90 km, this mountain range runs through 18 municipalities with villages that nestle in valleys among peaks that are often more than 1,000 m high, such as Puig Major (1,445 m) and Massanella (1,364 m). In 2011 the entire area was awarded World Heritage status by UNESCO in the Cultural Landscape category in recognition of the symbiosis between human beings and nature that has shaped this unique monumental work.

The land here has been used for subsistence activities over the centuries and their traces are clearly visible: kilometres of terraces whose boundaries are marked by drystone walls that reflect the titanic efforts to maintain the land and grow crops, which mainly consist of olive trees, some of them centuries old. Ancient paths, some of them cobbled, lead to chapels, sanctuaries, castles, charcoal furnaces and lime kilns. Also ice wells, where the ice dealers would store the ice for use in hospitals and noble houses.

Between the mountains, imposing estates, known as *possessions*, can be glimpsed. They were once major producers of olive oil and wool, with large flocks of sheep and goats, and were also used for dry-farming, growing carob, fig and almond trees, as well as irrigated crops, such as orange trees and vegetables. Ancient defence towers stand on the cliff-ridged coast. They formed an interconnecting network and were built to alert the villagers to pirate attacks.

The area is known for its varied landscapes, with chalky materials and limestone that have been converted into karstic formations as a result of the action of water. They crop out among wide swathes of pine and holm oak forests. The mountain range has ecosystems where a number of endemic botanical species thrive, such as the *Hypericum balearicum*, and it is also

The Serra de Tramuntana, World Heritage Site

Paratge Natural de la Serra de Tramuntana **Tramuntana**

a refuge for animals, such as the Mallorcan midwife toad (*Alytes muletensis*) and important bird species, such as the black vulture and Eleanora's falcon. The sea beds around the massif are covered in meadows of *Posidonia oceanica*, or Neptune grass, which plays a fundamental role in oxygenating the waters and breeding marine life.

The Serra de Tramuntana was declared an Area of Natural Beauty in 2007 and includes the Parc Natural de Sa Dragonera, several Natural Areas of Special Interest (ANEI), the marine reserves of Toro Island and the Illes Malgrats and the natural landmarks of the Torrent de Pareis and the Fonts Ufanes, underground sources that sprout suddenly in the middle of an oak grove after days of heavy rainfall.

Red crossbill (*Loxia curvirostra*)

GR-221

A popular, long-distance hiking trail through the landscapes of the Serra de Tramuntana taking in historic relics, villages and mountain huts. The route is 164 km long and well signposted. The main itinerary covers a distance of 91,7 km and there are 72,8 km of alternative paths.

Puig Major

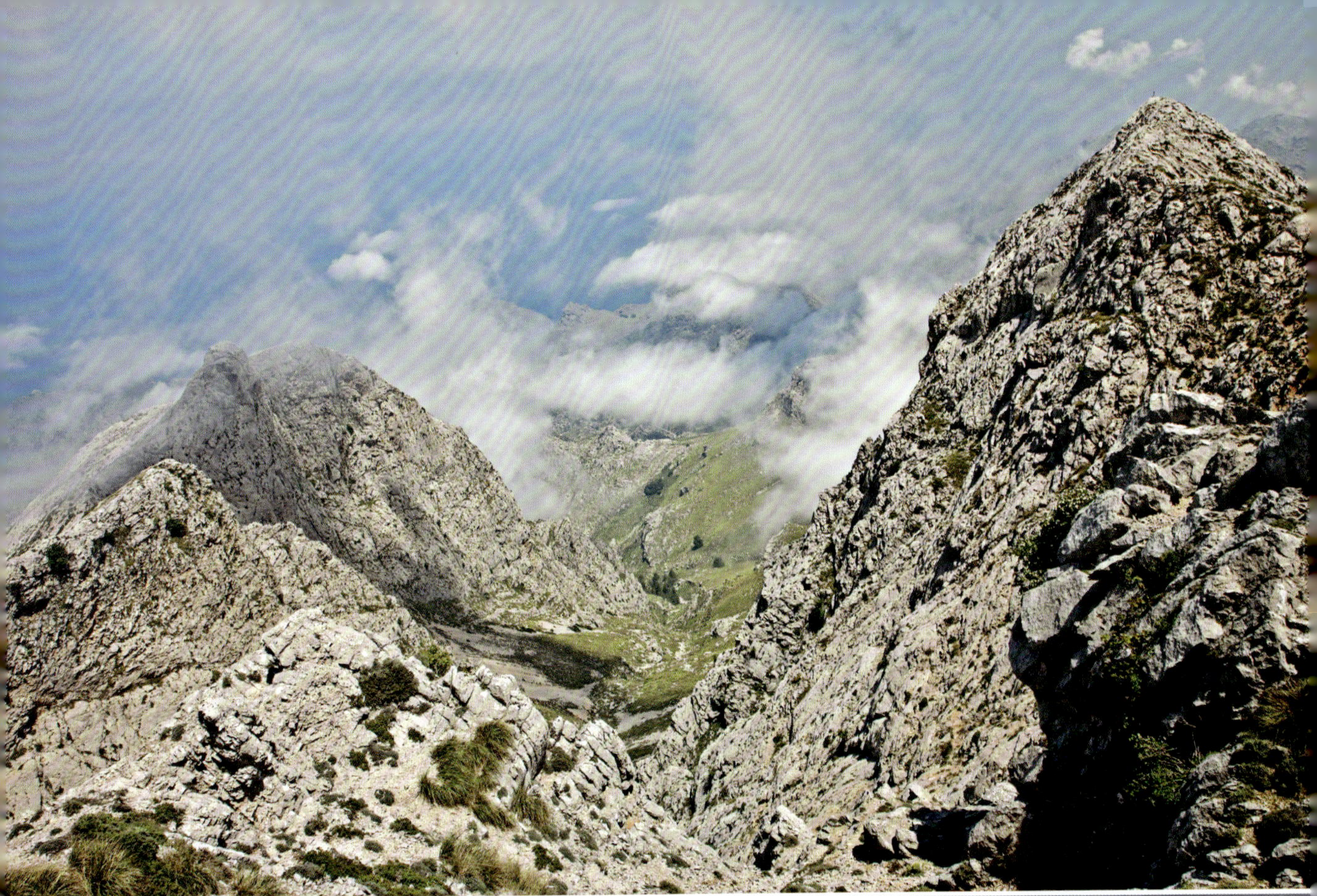
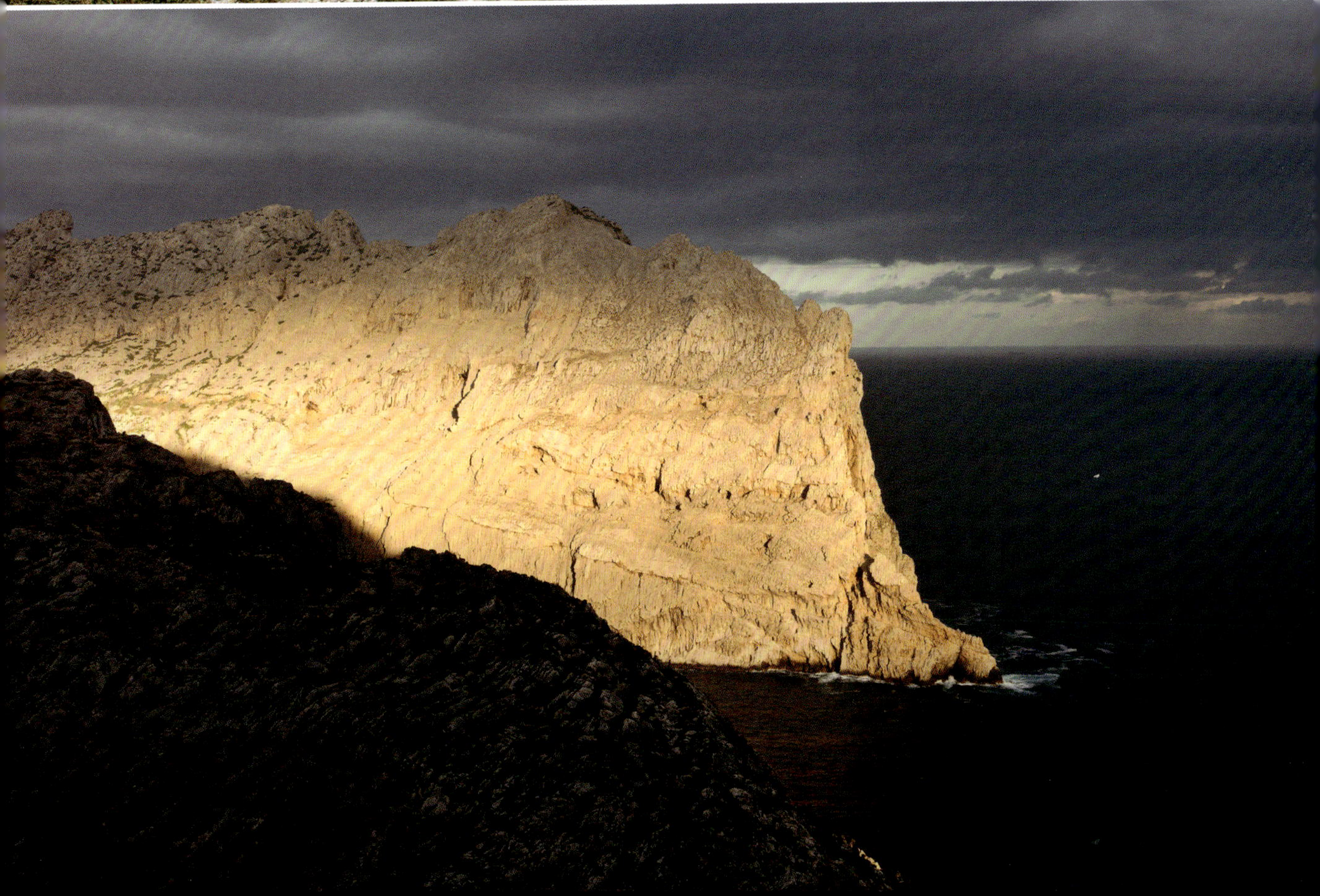

Formentor

Mallorcan wild goats (*Capra hircus*)

Formentor

Formentor is a narrow peninsula stretching for 12 km in the north of Mallorca, where the Serra de Tramuntana plunges dramatically down to the sea, forming cliffs up to 300 m high. A stunning landscape where the only sound you can hear is the crashing of the waves against the rocks. A winding road leads to peaceful beaches with a Mediterranean feel, such as Cala Pi de sa Posada. Unspoilt, wild, natural scenery that has inspired artists from around the world who have been drawn to its dizzying combination of magnetism and beauty.

Cap de Formentor

The winding road to the Formentor lighthouse begins in Port de Pollença. It stretches for 18 km and was built in 1925 by the engineer Antoni Parietti Coll (Palma, 1899-1979), who also supervised the construction of the Sa Calobra road. The most spectacular views of the Formentor cliffs can be enjoyed from the viewing point of Colomer, the Formentor lighthouse and the Albercuix defence tower which was built in the 16th century and stands 380 m above sea level. The tower formed a network with the others in Alcúdia and Pollença and they communicated with one another using smoke signals or fire. Today it boasts stunning vistas of the cliffs which are made even more beautiful by the solitary islet of El Colomer.

Cala Pi de sa Posada

A white, sandy beach with a Mediterranean feel, dotted with pines that edge the crystal-clear waters. In summer this is one of the most glamorous beaches on the island, partly due to the nearby luxury Hotel Formentor (today Formentor, a Royal Hideaway Hotel), which opened in 1929, and has included among its guests eminent personalities such as Churchill, the Dalai Lama, Chaplin, Audrey Hepburn, Gary Cooper and Peter Ustinov. The beach has a small landing stage for passengers on boats from Port de Pollença and the yachts that anchor in the Bay of Formentor.

The islet of El Colomer

Formentor lighthouse

Cala Pi de sa Posada

↑ Albercuix defence tower ↓ Cala Pi de Sa Posada

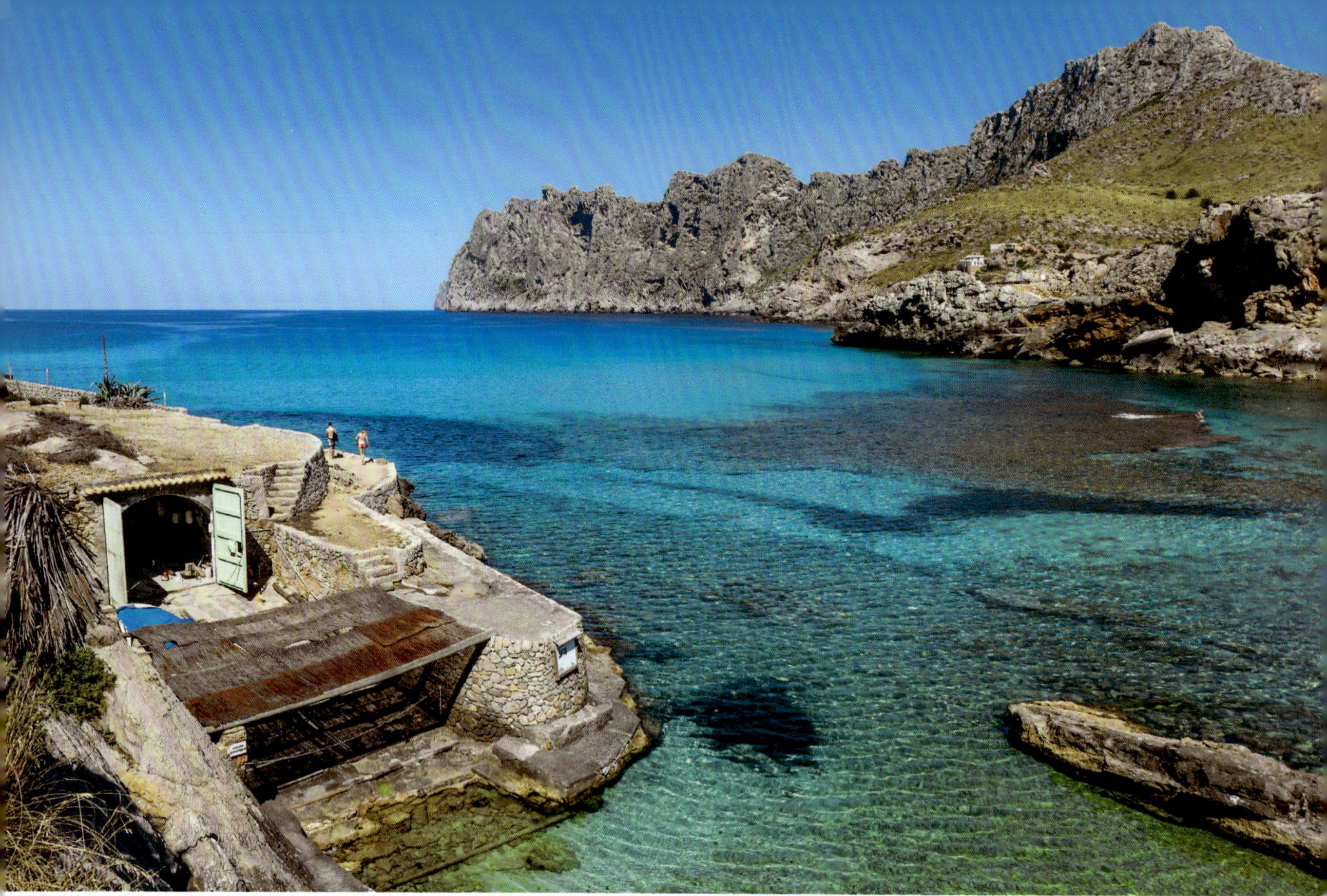

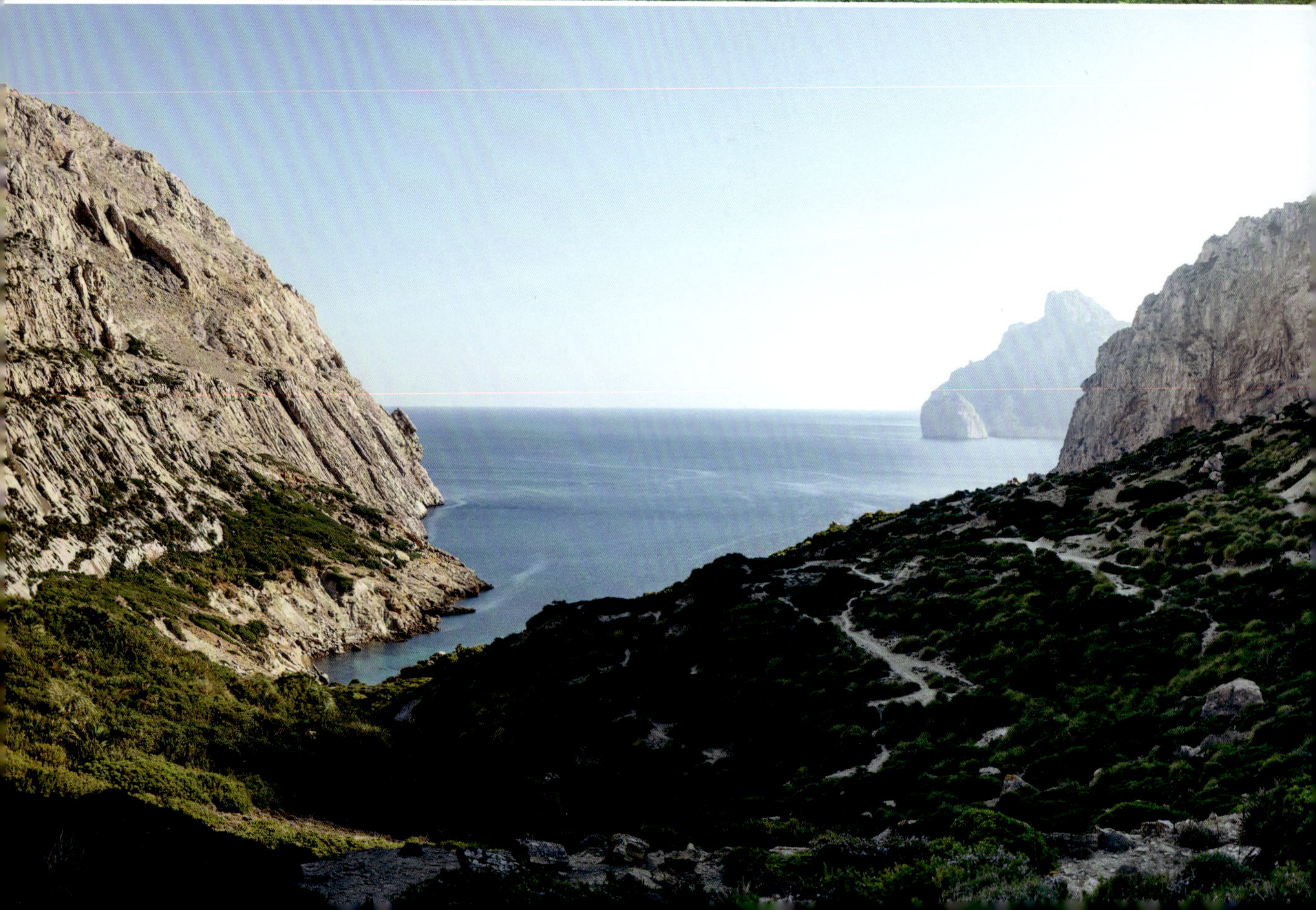

Cala Sant Vicent

This small tourist resort in the municipality of Pollença has developed around four tiny coves: Cala Varques, Cala Clara, Cala Molins and Cala Carbó. They are all equally beautiful with crystal-clear waters and are linked by a promenade. Although popular with summer holidaymakers, Cala Sant Vicenç is a peaceful spot, surrounded by chalets. The pre-talayotic caves of S'Alzineret are situated nearby, and it is the starting point for numerous hiking and bike trails. It is the perfect destination for families with children and lovers of water sports, as well as excellent restaurants to taste fish and seafood beside the sea. An enclave frequented by birds and ornithologists from around the world.

Cala Castell

An isolated, unspoilt cove with limpid waters that takes its name from the castle, the Castell del Rei, perched 476 m above the sea on a rocky cliff which is part of the mountain range, the Serra de Ternelles. The castle, which has stood guard over this stretch of the mountain range since the 13th century, can't be reached from the Serra de Tramuntana.

Cala Bóquer

Another unspoilt cove in a secluded inlet where the sea comes in for 300 m to create a wild, rugged and stunning landscape. Limestone cliffs rise up on both sides, with sparse vegetation, and the remains of the marine plant *Posidonia*, or Neptune grass, have been washed up on its shores, with their boulders and gravel. An enclave frequented by birds and ornithologists from around the world.

Cala Castell

Cala Molins

↖ Cala Sant Vicent
← Cala Bóquer

The bays of Pollença and Alcúdia

Bay of Pollença

The bays of Pollença and Alcúdia

Two broad sea inlets that have become one of the island's favourite spots due to its string of long, sandy beaches and nature reserves such as S'Albufereta and S'Albufera, wetlands and canals which are a stopping point for countless species of migratory birds. Further inland are the centuries-old towns of Pollença, Alcúdia, Muro and Santa Margalida, which show off their vast cultural and natural heritage with pride. The area has been inhabited for centuries, as evinced by the ruins of the Roman city of Pollentia (2nd century BC) and the Son Real necropolis (7th century BC).

Pollença

Pollença is a town and its old quarter features imposing stone houses, veritable palaces which look austere from the outside. The town began to grow in the 13th century around the church of the Mare de Déu dels Àngels (Our Lady of the Angels), the town's patron saint. The church that stands today was built between 1714 and 1790. The Convent of Sant Domingo dates from the 16th century and is another landmark building. Every year, its beautiful baroque cloisters are a venue for the prestigious Pollença Music Festival. Opposite the convent stand the Jardins Joan March, with their medieval Gothic tower and a statue dedicated to local hero, Joan Mas, who led the villagers in a fight against 1,500 Arabic pirates in the 16th century. Every summer the town stages a mock battle between Moors and Christians and all the locals join in. During the festivities there is dancing by *cossiers*, six men and a woman dressed in white who perform time-honoured dances. They are accompanied by the devil who tries to sabotage the dancing. A piece of high land, known as El Calvari, boasts the best views of the town. To get there, you have to go up a stairway consisting of 365 steps lined with cypress trees.

↑ **Plaça Major and Puig de Maria**   ↓ **Carrer del Calvari**

The Font del Gall

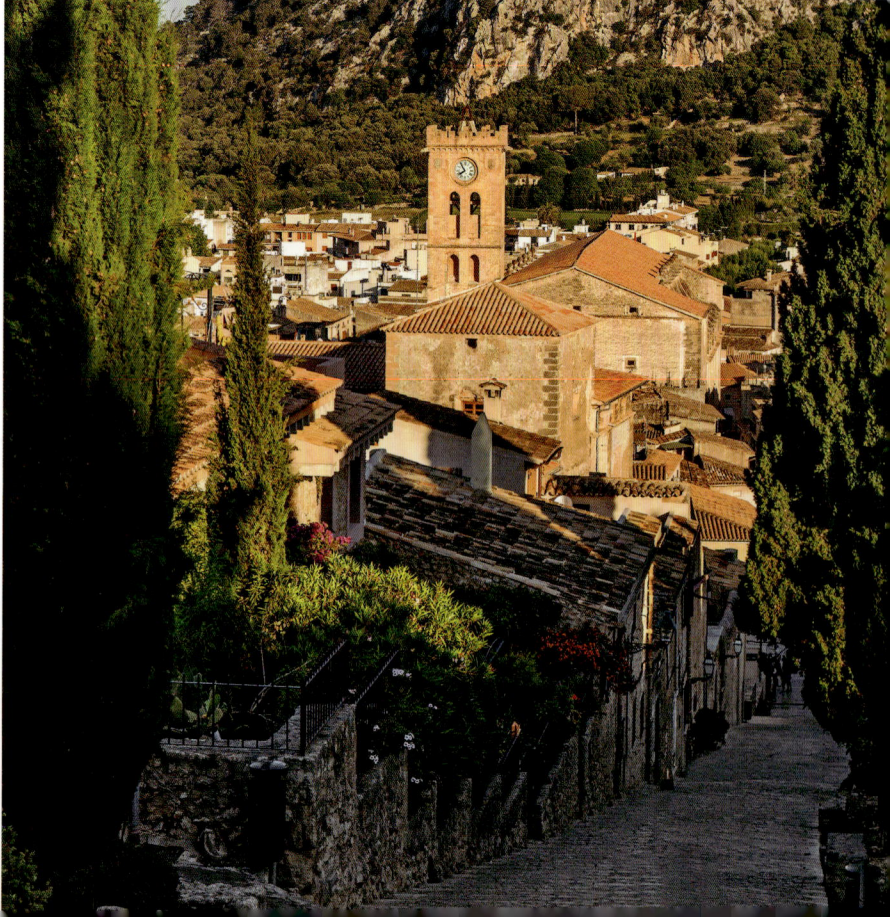

Pollença **The bays of Pollença and Alcúdia**

Port de Pollença

Port de Pollença, which is known by the local residents as Moll (quay), was just a small fishing village until the early 20th century. Today it has become a popular tourist resort that still retains its family atmosphere, as many islanders bought their holiday homes here. There is a long promenade along the seafront, which is popular with walkers, cyclists and sports lovers. Some parts enjoy welcome shade from the old pine trees, their roots anchored firmly in the sand. Fishing boats and small wooden vessels, known as *llaüts*, berth in the old harbour in stark contrast to the huge yachts at the modern sailing club, the Club Nàutic. A fine place for enjoying the seafaring dishes such as paella and lobster stew.

The bay seen from the Bellresguard complex **Port de Pollença**

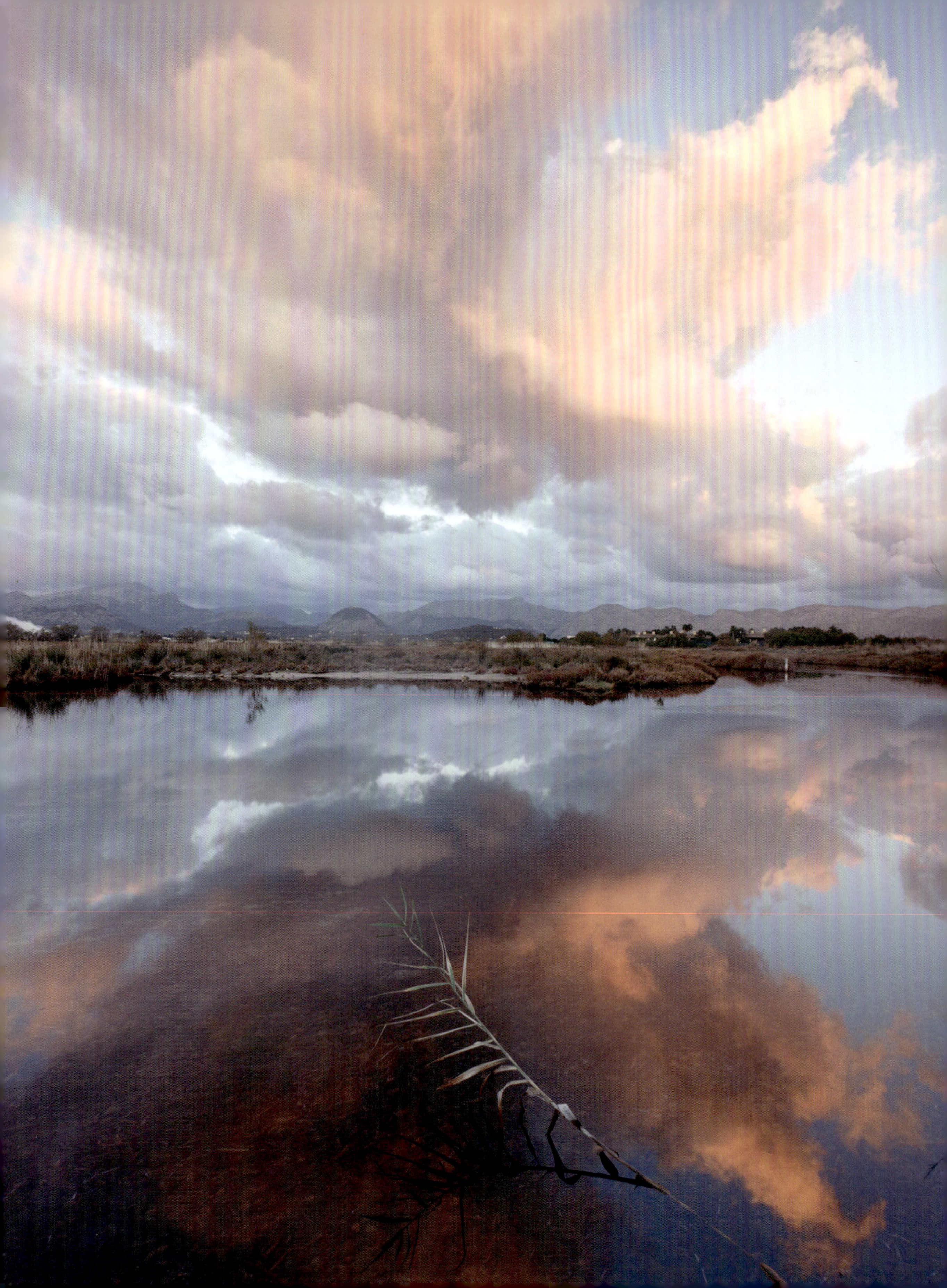

Reserva Natural de S'Albufereta

One of the jewels in the Bay of Pollença, S'Albufereta is a wetland area of canals and marshes comprising more than 200 ha that are a designated protected Natural Reserve and a Natural Area of Special Interest (ANEI). It is a key site for many water birds during their yearly migrations and a haven for countless species during the recurrent dry spells that are characteristic of Mediterranean summers. Bird watchers from around the world travel the length and breadth of the reserve on foot or by bike to observe cormorants, herons, coots and moorhens or get a fleeting glimpse of Eleanora's falcon or an osprey hunting their prey.

Due to its proximity to the sea, Albufereta abounds with plants that are typical of wetland areas with high salinity levels. These include glasswort prairies, tamarisk groves and one of the most important tamarisk forests on Mallorca. The insect community is at times scarcely visible, and includes dragonflies, praying mantis and a number of butterfly species.

The El Rec stream is the main source of water in S'Albufereta. An almost permanent water course, it is supplied by the springs known as the Ulls de Rec which are a mixture of salt and fresh water. Water in the reserve also comes from the torrents of Can Xanet and Can Roig and the source known as the Font del Mal Any.

In times past, the land on S'Albufereta was an important agricultural reserve and some of the properties are still involved in farming, with fields that are also frequented by goldfinches, sparrows, kestrels and egrets.

Common tern (*Sterna hirundo*)

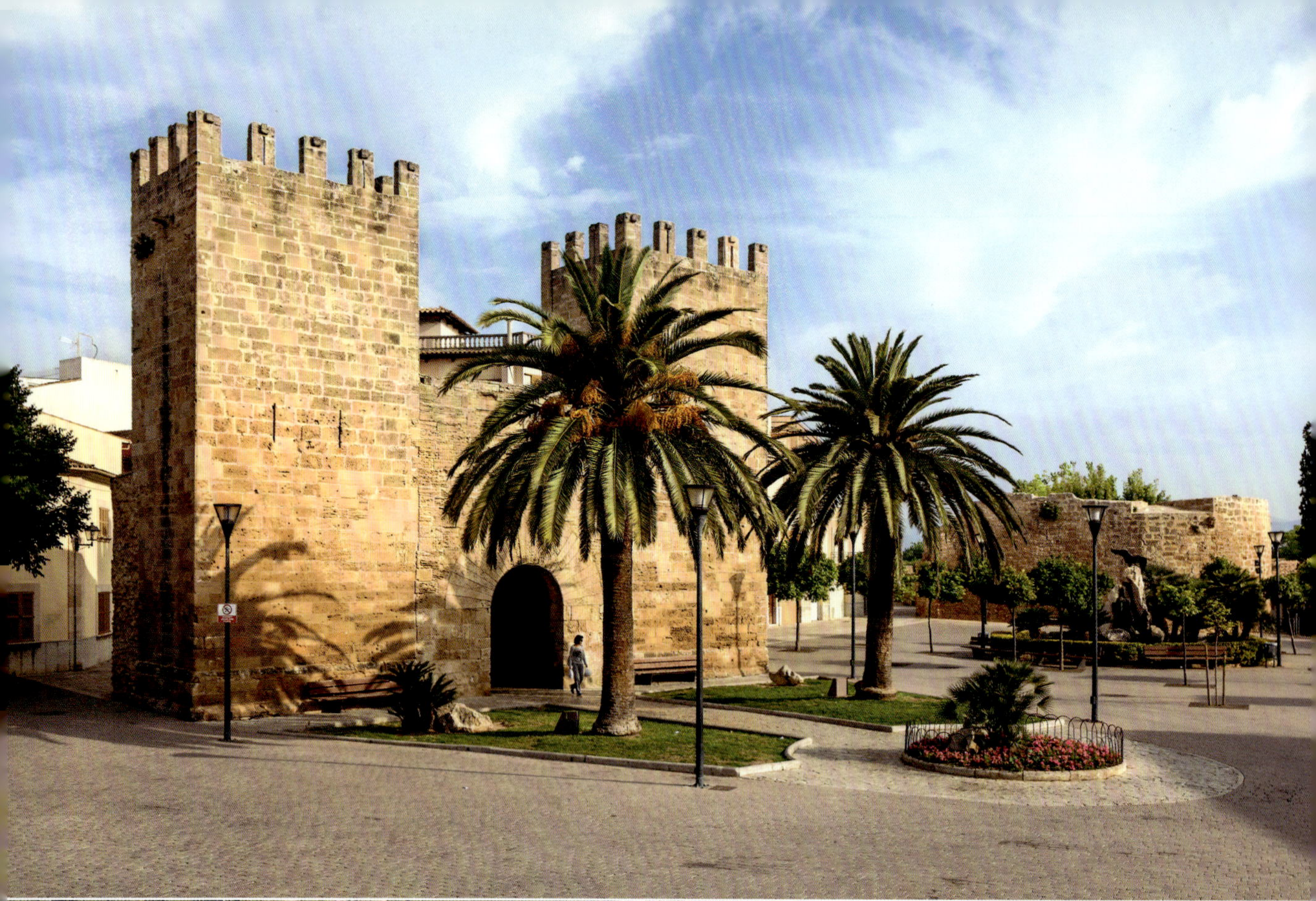

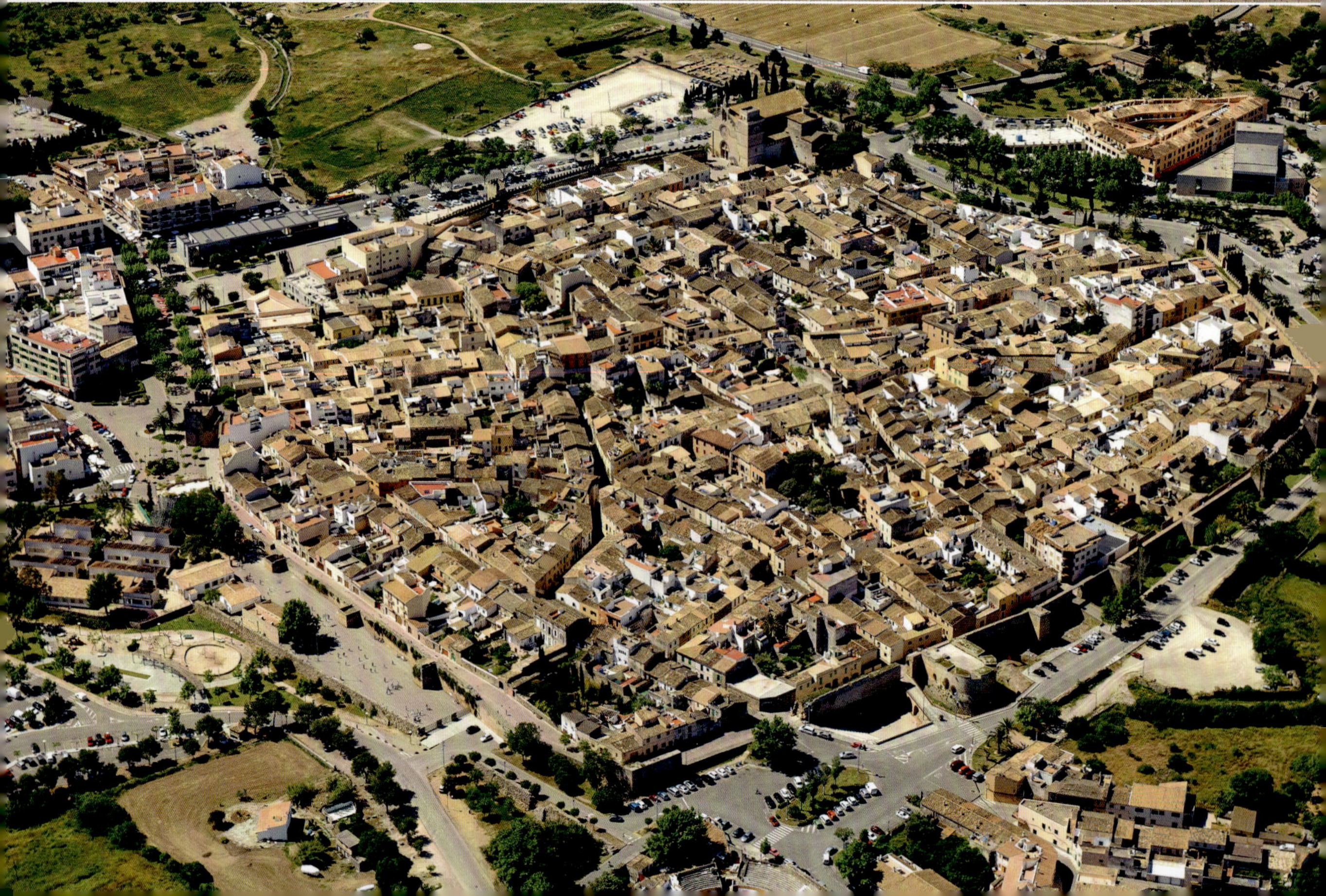

Alcúdia

This historic town welcomes its visitors with the impressive sight of its ancient ramparts, built by King Jaume II in the 14th century to protect the townsfolk and possesses a stronghold in the event of an attack. The ramparts had a quadrangular structure made up of 26 towers set out along a 1,500-metre perimeter. In the 16th century they were reinforced by three bulwarks. Inside the walled town is the original part of the settlement, with ancient mansions that underwent alterations in the 16th century, such as the addition of Renaissance-style elements in accordance with the style of the times. Some of them have been converted into restaurants, hotels and cultural amenities, such as Can Torró, which is now a magnificent public library.

Pollentia

Alcúdia is also home to the archaeological remains of the Roman town of Pollentia. Founded in the 2nd century BC by the consul Quintus Caecilius Metellus, it still retains buildings such as the theatre, the forum, the Capitoline Temple and an area of taverns. The most important finds are on display at the Museu Monogràfic de Pollentia, facing the church of Sant Jaume.

Church of Sant Jaume

Bell tower of the town hall

↖ Port of El Moll
← Walled town of Alcúdia

Roman city of Pollentia

Es Barcarès and Es Mal Pas

The town of Alcúdia has grown to the north with housing developments where many Mallorcans have chosen to set up their holiday homes attracted by their seafront location. Es Barcarés overlooks the Bay of Pollença with a beautiful beach that can be reached on foot. It never gets busy and is a welcoming spot popular with families. The sandy shoreline is perfect for a barefoot paddle in the crystal-clear waters. Es Mal Pas is another residential area near the almost identical beaches of Sant Pere and Sant Joan. It has a diverse population and in recent years the number of German and British residents has increased, some of whom have chosen this part of the island to live all year round.

Alcanada

Words can't possibly do justice to the beauty of this enclave: a tiny beach bathed by crystal-clear waters with boulders and gravel where ancient pines grow providing much-needed shade in summer. On the horizon you can see the small island of Alcanada, with a lighthouse as its centrepiece.

Sant Pere

Locals and summer holidaymakers from Es Mal Pas frequent this beach overlooking the Bay of Pollença which boasts views of Formentor in the distance. Stretching for more than 100 m, its shores of fine, white sand back onto a leafy pine glade and have a pleasant family atmosphere.

Sant Joan

The beaches of Sant Joan and Sant Pere make up a pigeon pair and are connected by a short, rocky path. Sant Joan has limpid waters that are the perfect place for swimming and diving and popular with families looking for a peaceful spot for a day by the sea. At the back of the beach is a slope covered with vegetation that is perfectly suited to the salt and the wind.

Es Barcarès

Alcanada

Sant Pere and Sant Joan beaches

Platja de Muro

Muro is a vast beach between Casetes des Capellans, a coastal village of low-rise houses and sandy streets, and the small beach of Es Braç. Stretching for 5.2 km, it is one of the wildest and most unspoilt beaches in the Bay of Alcúdia. Its fine sands are dotted with juniper and pine forests that make up a valuable dune system extending some distance inland. The area known as Es Comú has been declared a Natural Area of Special Interest, and is part of the Parc Natural de S'Albufera. Its waters are shallow and have a moderate swell making them popular among families with children who enjoy all the facilities and amenities on offer.

Mallorcan baskets on sale at a market on the coast

Muro beach

Santa Margalida
Can Picafort

Long ago, Can Picafort was a fishing village surrounded by long beaches. Over the years, it has become a major tourism hub and today it offers more than 10,000 hotel beds and a wide range of services that are enjoyed in summer by visitors, most of them from Germany and the UK. Many people live at the resort throughout the year and it has four beaches: Sa Platja Gran, Son Bauló, Son Real and Son Serra de Marina. The latter is completely unspoilt and stretches for 400 m. Popular with windsurfers, paddle surfers and people who enjoy all kinds of water sports Can Picafort boasts views of the majestic cape Cap Ferrutx which stands on the easternmost tip of the Bay of Alcúdia.

Son Real

This public estate stands almost in the centre of the Bay of Alcúdia. Covering an area of about 400 hectares people have lived here since prehistoric times. Evidence of human activity dating back 4,500 years has been found here, along with finds from the pre-talayotic era (4,000 years), talayotic era (3,000 years), Roman era (more than 2,000 years), Islamic, medieval and contemporary eras. Arguably the most important are the prehistoric cemeteries, or necropolises, on the islet, the Illot des Porros, and the headland, the Punta des Fenicis, which have been exposed to the waves for centuries.

Sa Platja Gran

Punta des Fenicis necropolis

Horse trekking through the public estate of Son Real

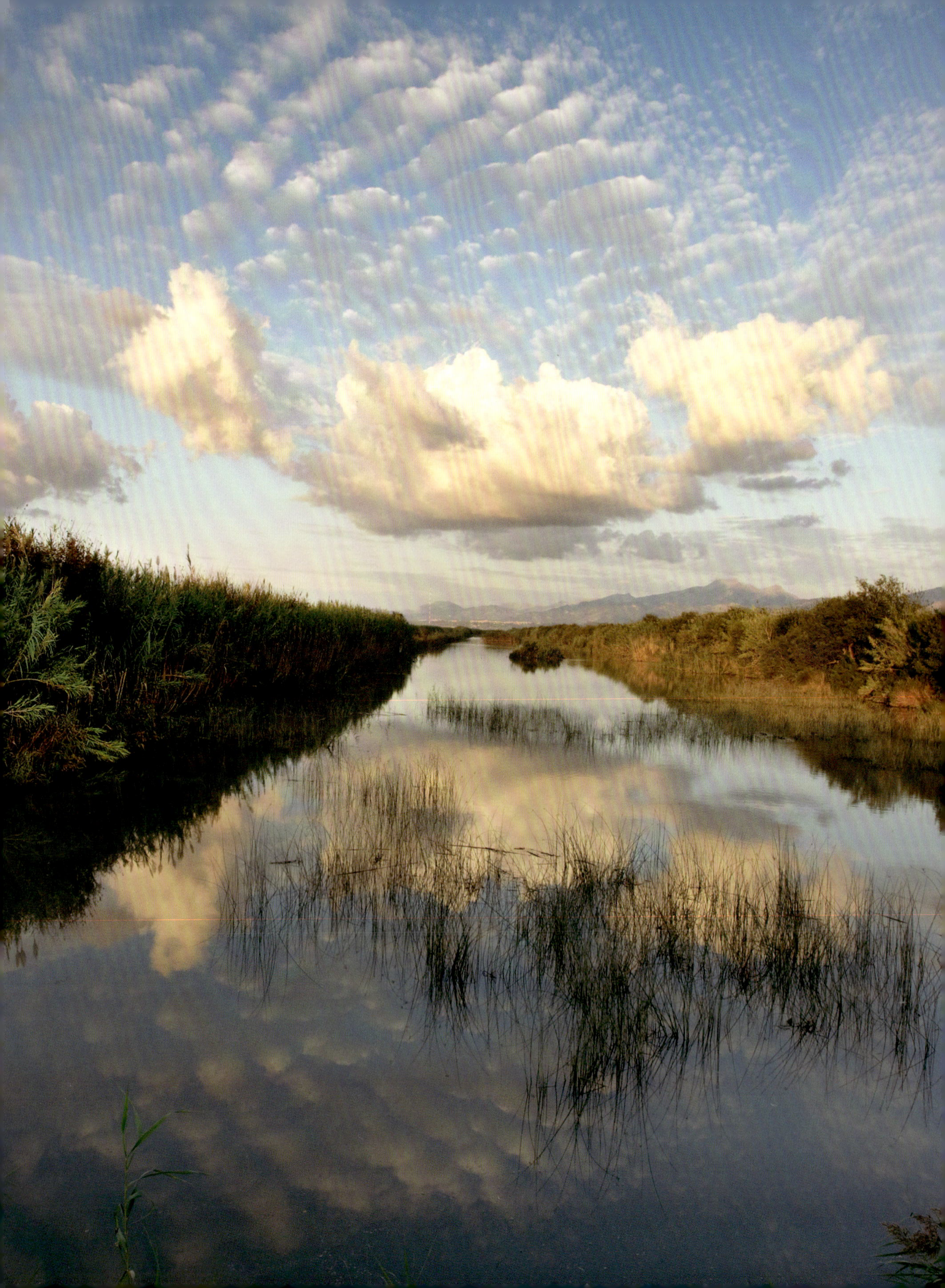

Parc Natural de S'Albufera de Mallorca — The bays of Pollença and Alcúdia

Parc Natural de S'Albufera de Mallorca

A paradise for thousands of birds who find shelter and food in the wetlands and canals of S'Albufera. Water forms the biological basis of the wetland: the wet soil favours the growth of plants that varies according to the depth of the water, closeness to the sea and type of land. Much of its water comes from freshwater torrents, underground aquifers and rainfall, while in summer, seawater intrusion still has an effect on the flora and fauna. A wide variety of plants and trees grow on the banks, including white poplars, elms and tamarisks.

A wealth of species live in the water, including eels, and amphibians abound, among them the common frog and reptiles such as the water snake. On land, there is also space for mammals to thrive hers, particularly bats, mice and rats. There are also countless invertebrates, with numerous species of dragonflies, beetles and moths.

However, birds are the noisiest and most spectacular group in the natural park. More than 300 species that stop over in summer have been identified, and some of them breed here. More than 10,000 birds winter in S'Albufera, and visitors will have no difficulty in finding ducks, herons and groups of starlings. Migratory birds, such as teal and swallows, stop off here for short periods of time. There are also species that are occasional visitors, such as cranes. There are a number of signposted footpaths and cycle paths with hides and observation platforms for birdwatching.

Mallard (*Anas platyrhynchos*)

Great Crested Grebe (*Podiceps cristatus*)

Península de Llevant

Cala Agulla

Península de Llevant

This area of land, in north-east Mallorca, is shared by the municipalities of Artà and Capdepera, and combines the charms of the mountains —the Serres de Llevant massif— and the sea, a string of coves with shimmering, turquoise waters, including Cala Estreta, Cala Mesquida and Cala Agulla, and tourist resorts like Cala Rajada. The villages treasure and take pride in their heritage, which includes landmarks such as the castle of Capdepera, a fortress that played a crucial role in defending the island in the 14th century. There are also places that are highly prized by hikers and nature lovers who enjoy several signposted routes that go through the Parc Natural de la Península de Llevant.

Artà

Artà nestles in a wide valley crowned by a hill, the Puig de Sant Salvador, which has a walled precinct and a popular sanctuary at the top. The town has been inhabited since prehistoric times and is surrounded by important archaeological sites, such as Ses Païsses. During the Muslim era, it was one of Mallorca's 13 districts and was known as Yartân, which is the origin of its present name.

Stone mansions abound in the old town, examples of traditional architecture that coexist with contemporary buildings such as the Teatre d'Artà, a cultural hub that attracts people from all over the island. Many local craftspeople have workshops in the town and produce pottery, textiles, silver and gold work using traditional methods and practise an ancient craft known as *llata*, which consists of making objects from dried palmetto fronds. The palmetto, or fan palm, is native to Mallorca and the craft has always been the domain of women, its secrets passed down from generation to generation to make baskets, bags and accessories.

The festival of Sant Antoni, held on the night of 16th January, are very popular: the locals light huge bonfires, or *foguerons*, and share a meal and the most skilful poets make up verses.

Wall around L'Almudaina

Traditional Mallorcan folk tales at Artartà

Street in the city centre

↑ L'Almudaina ↓ Church of Els Pares Franciscans

Parc Natural de la Península de Llevant

A nature reserve covering 1,671 ha that protects a large area of the mountains in and around Artà and includes the highest peaks on the Serres de Llevant, including Puig Morei (564 m) and Puig des Porrassar (491 m). The protected territory also includes the nature reserves of Cap de Ferrutx and Cap des Freu, two areas of unspoilt cliffs.

The landscape is largely the result of the centuries-old interaction between human beings and nature. There are still farmsteads with olive and almond groves, as well as fig and carob trees. In bygone years, livestock farming was an important activity that left its mark on the landscape: vast swathes of woodland and scrubland were burned to create new pastures for sheep and goats, thereby fostering species that grew back easily, such as reeds and palmettos. Although the reeds have encroached on large areas of land, the park also has coastal cliffs, caves, chasms, woodland and torrents.

Many species endemic to the Balearic Islands can be found among the park's botanical treasures. These include the Balearic St John's wort (*Hypericum balearicum*). There are also endemic animal species, including the snail *Iberellus balearicus*, as well as large numbers of Mediterranean tortoises, hedgehogs, genets and pine martens. The bird species include sparrowhawks, peregrine falcons, Audouin's gulls and cormorants.

The architectural heritage is a key feature of the site. Highlights include the Moreia watchtower, the remains of a republican prisoner of war camp from the Spanish Civil War, houses that were part of noble estates, drystone walls, mills and cisterns.

S'Arenalet d'Albarca

Moreia watchtower

Betlem coast →

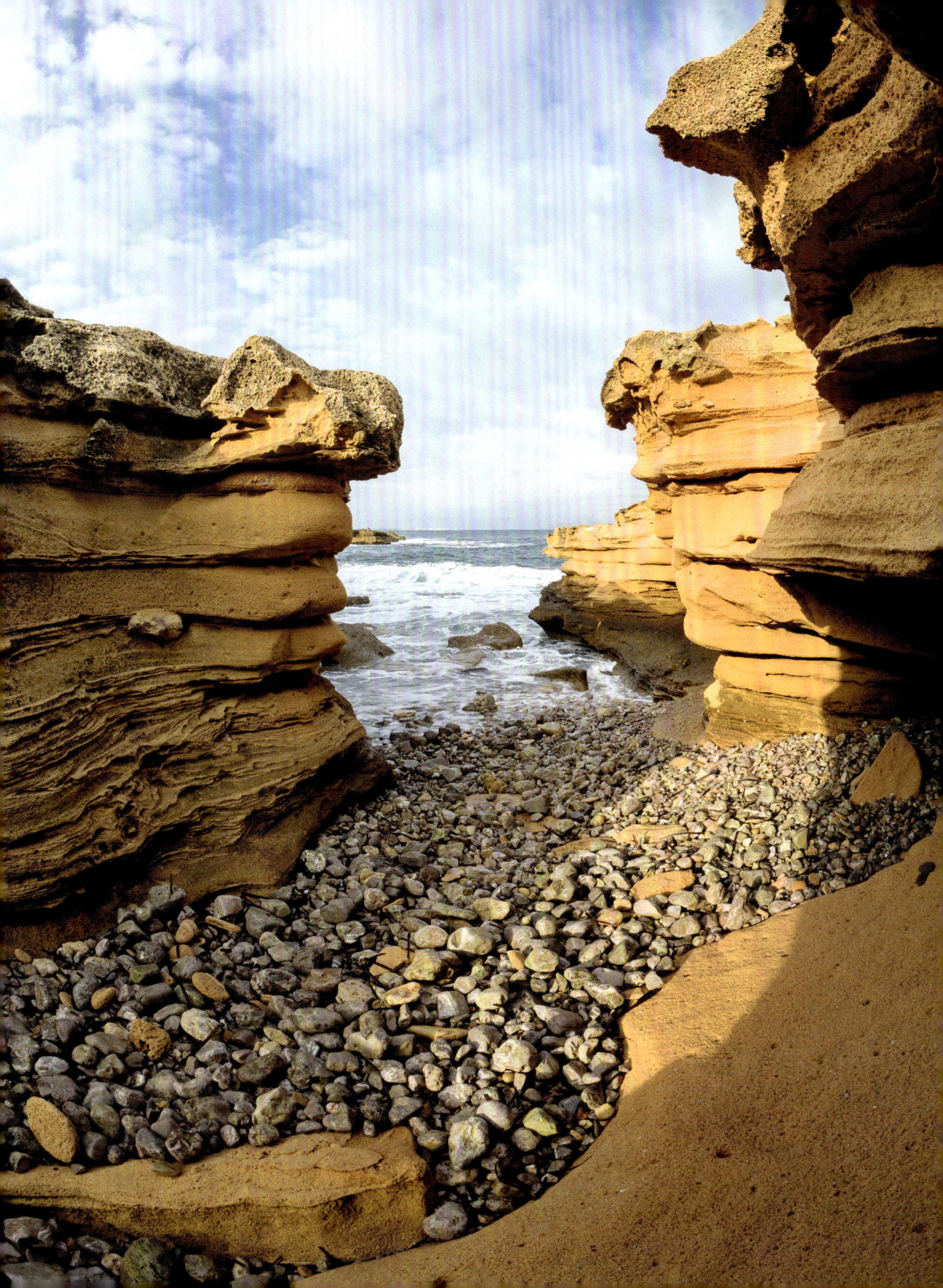

Colònia de Sant Pere
Betlem-Sa Canova

The Colònia de Sant Pere is a small coastal village founded in the 19th century when a group of families moved here to devote themselves to farming and fishing. An island within an island, it remains a peaceful spot and a popular summer holiday destination for many families on the island who love its pleasant, tranquil seaside atmosphere. Holiday complexes, such as Betlem, Montferrutx and S'Estanyol, started to be built nearby in the 1960s. The most popular local beach is Sa Canova, or Areny de Sa Canova. Enclosed by the headland, the Punta de Sa Barraca, and the Na Borges torrent, it has fine sand and an impressive dune system.

Chapel of Betlem

This chapel stands on land once occupied by the ancient Muslim farmstead of Binialgorfa. It was founded in 1805 by members of the hermit communities of Saint Honoratus from Randa and the Holy Trinity of Valldemossa. Around the chapel are the remains of ancient allotments, a threshing floor and buildings associated with the self-sufficient monastic life.

Sa Canova

Chapel of Betlem

View of Cap Ferrutx from the Artà Massif

S'Arenalet d'Albarca and Sa Font Celada

These beautiful unspoilt beaches can only be reached by land or after walking more than 5 km through the Parc Natural de la Península de Llevant. Their inaccessibility has protected them from any human impact, meaning that they consist of unique, wild landscapes that allow us to imagine what Mallorca was like before the days of mass tourism. S'Arenalet comprises a long strip of sand bathed by crystal-clear waters, while Sa Font Celada, at the mouth of Es Castellot torrent, is a deep coastal inlet surrounded by sparse vegetation. Peaceful beaches for people who love walking, solitude and silence broken only by the murmur of the waves.

Cala Torta, Cala Mitjana, Cala Estreta and Es Matzoc

These are four of the best beaches in Artà. At 150 m long and 100 m wide, Cala Torta is the largest beach in the municipality and has fine, white sand. Cala Mitjana backs on to a small dune system and is surrounded by lush pine groves. Cala Estreta is a narrow and deep inlet bathed by shimmering, emerald waters. And Es Matzoc, with its fine sand and boulders, has an 18th century defence tower with its cannon intact from where the islanders kept a mistrustful eye on British Menorca. Beaches bounded by rocky sandstone outcrops formed by the grains of sand from fossil dunes dating back millions of years.

S'Arenalet d'Albarca

Cala Estreta

Cala Torta

Capdepera

The history of Capdepera dates back to 1300, when King Jaume II issued a decree ordering a village to be built starting with a church surrounded by a wall inside which the islanders would live. The church, the wall and its towers have survived the passing of the centuries and are now one of the most important historic sites on Mallorca. Capdepera Castle, which can be seen from anywhere in the town, was a strategic enclave where the islanders would seek refuge and defend themselves from attacks. As the years went by, the population grew and spread beyond the walls. In the 19th century, Capdepera became an independent municipality.

The walls had a semi-triangular layout with four towers: Des Costerans, Sa Boira, Ses Dames and En Banya. The governor's house, the Casa del Gobernador, stood within the walls. Today it houses the Museu de la Llata, which is dedicated to the history and secrets of the traditional Mallorcan art of weaving palmetto fronds. The Torre de En Miquel Nunis, which is Arabic in origin, stands at the highest point of the town. In the 19th century it housed a flour mill. Nearby is the tiny church where you can see a Gothic carving of Christ made from orange wood. In May, Capdepera goes back to the Middle Ages with a medieval fair where you'll find a wide variety of handmade products and displays of ancient trades and crafts.

View of the wall of Capdepera Castle

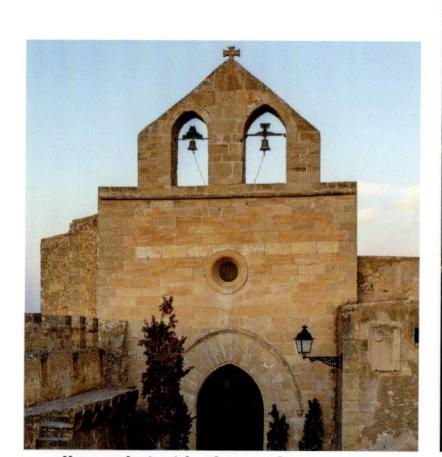

Small temple inside the castle

Church of Capdepera

Capdepera **Península de Llevant**

Cala Rajada
At the beginning of the 20th century, this former fishing village became a favourite summer holiday haunt for well-to-do families. The Capdepera lighthouse was built here in the middle of the 19th century amid a rugged landscape of cliffs from where the island of Menorca could be glimpsed on clear days. Today Cala Rajada is a major resort with numerous hotels and restaurants where you can sample fresh fish right by the sea. During the festival of the Verge del Carme, or Our Lady of Carmen, the patron saint of sailors, the port is the setting for a popular procession of boats. In October the town celebrates the Mostra de la Llampuga, during which chefs and restaurants make dishes from *llampuga*, or dolphinfish, a species that appears off the coast from September onwards.

Cala Rajada

Dolphinfish with red peppers

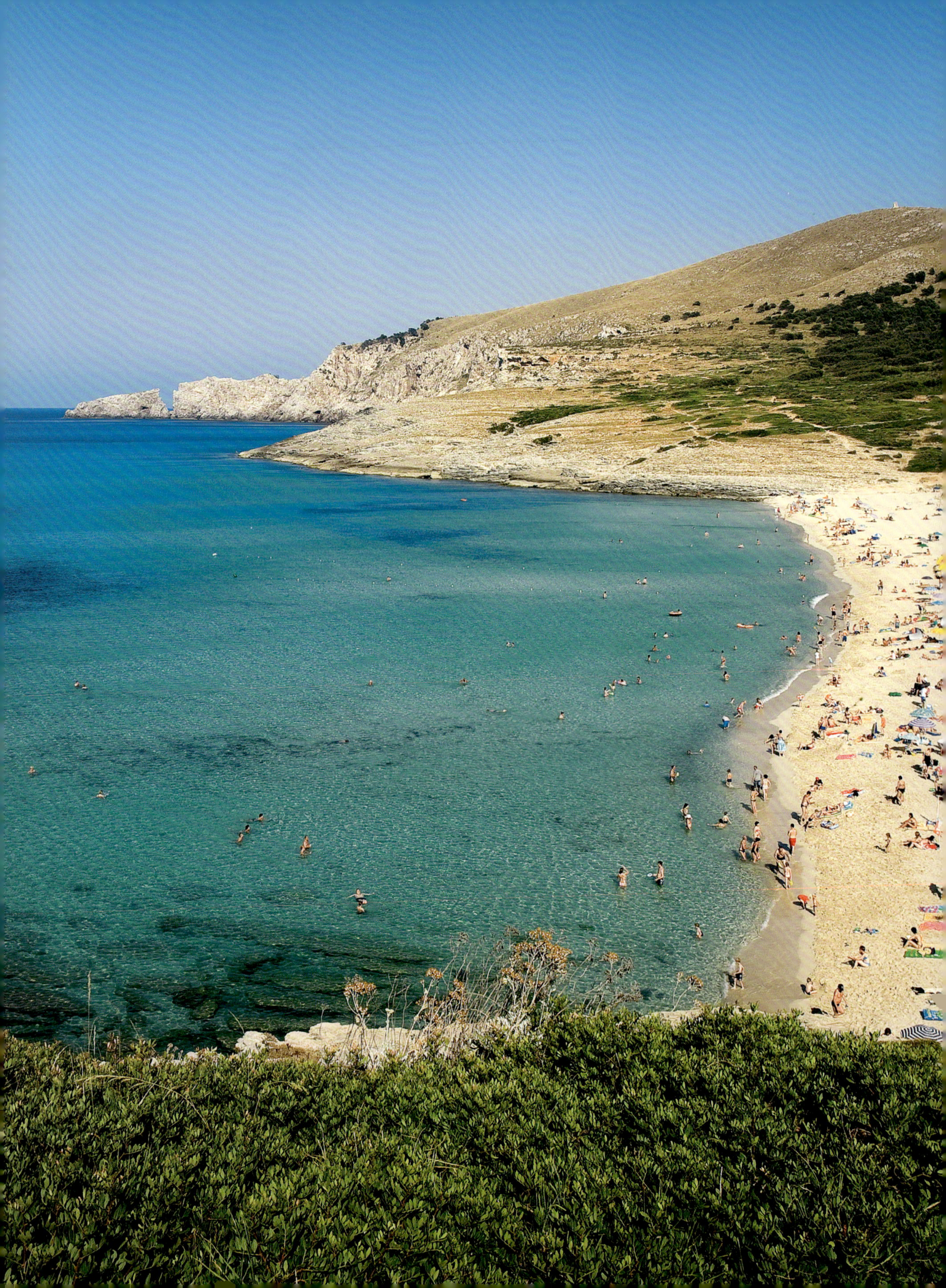

Península de Llevant

Cala Mesquida

The name Cala Mesquida, or S'Arenal de Sa Mesquida, is taken from the nearby estate, Sa Mesquida de Dalt. This beach, together with the neighbouring Cala Moltó and Cala Agulla, is a designated Natural Area of Special Interest. It has a wide strip of fine sand set among low cliffs and backs onto a dune system with a profusion of mastic trees and pines. A large colony of gulls and cormorants lives on the right shore which has no buildings. This is a dangerous place to swim when northerly, north-easterly and north-westerly winds are blowing as they create big waves.

Sa Font de Sa Cala

This small tourist resort is located just 2 km from Cala Rajada and takes its name from a nearby freshwater stream. Undersea run-off also flows out into the sea here, meaning that the water is colder and less brackish than elsewhere on the coast. The beach used to have boulders but sand has been brought in to create a man-made beach which is considerably larger than it originally was. The holiday complexes of Cala Provençal and Es Carregador have been built around the resort.

Cala Gat

A beautiful cove with a sandy beach below Sa Torre Cega, which was built as a defence tower to keep watch for marauding pirates. In 1911 it was converted into a palace with a sculpture park, showcasing a unique collection of sculptures, and a botanical gardens covering an area of 60,000 m².

Canyamel

A peaceful tourist resort nestling between two capes: Cap Vermell and Cap des Pinar. Its name originates from the sugar cane that was grown widely in this area. In addition to its long beaches, other attractions include the Artà caves and the 13th-century Torre de Canyamel.

Sa Font de Sa Cala

Cala Gat

← Cala Mesquida

Canyamel

Llevant

Cala Varques

Llevant

Located further inland, in the east of Mallorca, the county of Llevant follows the contours of the Serres de Llevant mountain range. Nearby, you'll find the historic town of Manacor —which is famous for its furniture and artificial pearls— and Felanitx which is renowned for its wines. On the coast, erosion of the limestone by the sea has created a succession of coves that have remained well preserved due to complicated access by land. And tourist resorts have been established in old fishing ports, such as Cala Bona and Portocristo, with sandy beaches and attractions such as the caves, the Coves del Drach, which have one of the biggest underwater lakes in Europe.

Sa Marjal and Es Ribell
Sa Marjal and Es Ribell make up a long beach of white, fine sand which is the longest in the Bay of Son Servera. Nestling between Sa Punta de N'Amer and Cap des Pinar, it is the only beach on the Costa dels Pins that hasn't been overbuilt, although luxurious mansions can be glimpsed among the pines.

Cala Bona
A tiny resort with a fishing harbour where the traditional Mediterranean boats known as *llaüts* still moor. They are between 3 and 5 m long and are now powered by diesel. The beach has all kinds of amenities and services as well as bars with terraces where you can soak up the laid-back atmosphere.

Cala Millor
A tourist resort spread between two municipalities, Sant Llorenç des Cardassar and Son Servera. The fine, sandy beach bathed by crystal-clear waters is almost 2 km long and is a great place for a leisurely stroll or windsurfing, paddle surfing or diving.

Cala Millor

Neptune grass (*Posidonia oceanica*)

Cala Bona

Punta de N'Amer

Sa Punta de N'Amer is a tiny peninsula that juts out into the sea between the resorts of Sa Coma and Cala Millor. Covering some 200 ha, it has been named a Natural Area of Special Interest (ANEI) due to its outstanding scenery and cultural attractions. These include a 17th century defence tower, Es Castell, with a square base, disused sandstone quarries and bunkers dating from the Spanish Civil War (1936-1939). Although it only covers a small area, Punta de N'Amer offers a rich and varied landscape: dunes, fields of crops, savin juniper and pine glades. It has one of the best viewing points overlooking the eastern coast of Mallorca.

Sa Coma

A purpose-built resort with hotels and housing complexes built in the 1980s around Sa Coma beach. Stretching for more than 800 m, its fine, white sands are bathed by crystal-clear waters and overlook the beautiful headland, the Punta de N'Amer. You can cycle along the bike lane between Cala Millor and S'Illot.

S'Illot

S'Illot became a favourite a summer holiday spot with Manacor locals during the 1930s. Situated by the beaches of Cala Moreia, Cala Morlanda and Caló d'En Rafalino, people have lived here for centuries. This is borne out by the prehistoric settlement of S'Illot which was established in 2,200 BC and inhabited until the 2nd century AD.

Punta de N'Amer

Sa Coma

S'Illot

Portocristo

This former fishing village is situated inside a long, sheltered inlet. It has a fine, sandy beach and shallow waters and is enclosed at one end by the promontory Es Morro de Sa Carabassa, which has a lighthouse at the top dating from 1851. There are numerous hotels, bars, restaurants and a large shopping area.

Coves del Drach and Coves dels Hams

The caves known as the Coves del Drach, and the Coves dels Hams, with its formations reminiscent of fish hooks ("hams" in Catalan) are located deep in the bowels of Mallorca. The former were first explored in 1896 by the caver Martel, who discovered the large underwater lake that today bears his name. It is 170 m long and up to 12 m deep.

Manacor

Manacor is Mallorca's most populous municipality after Palma and was awarded city status in 1912. The local museum preserves the relics of all the cultures that have settled here from the pre-talayotic era to the present day. Although Manacor's economy used to be based on livestock farming, agriculture and the textile sector, it is known today for the production of quality furniture and artificial pearls.

Portocristo

Plaça de Weyler

Manacor, church of Nostra Senyora dels Dolors

Portocristo | Manacor **Llevant** 105

Cala Mendia and Cala Anguila

These two sheltered coves, with their deep waters, stand barely 300 m apart. They both have sandy beaches and crystal-clear waters which, as the day progresses, take on shimmering turquoise and emerald hues. A large number of hotels and new residential neighbourhoods have sprung up around them.

Cala Varques

This unspoilt cove forms an almost rectangular inlet and is, in fact, made up of a large cove and another smaller one which are separated by a rocky breakwater. There are low cliffs on both sides with scant vegetation. The transparent waters reveal the white sandy seabed.

Cala Magraner, Cala Pilota and Cala Virgili

Three unspoilt coves that are part of a Natural Area of Special Interest and have been created by the action of the waves, torrents and wind on the limestone rocks. Plants that are perfectly adapted to brackish waters thrive on this coastal strip, and include species such as *Limonium biflorum*, known locally as *saladina*, and samphire.

Cala Anguila

Cala Varques

Cala Magraner, the biggest cove, Cala Pilota and Cala Virgili

Coves del Drach

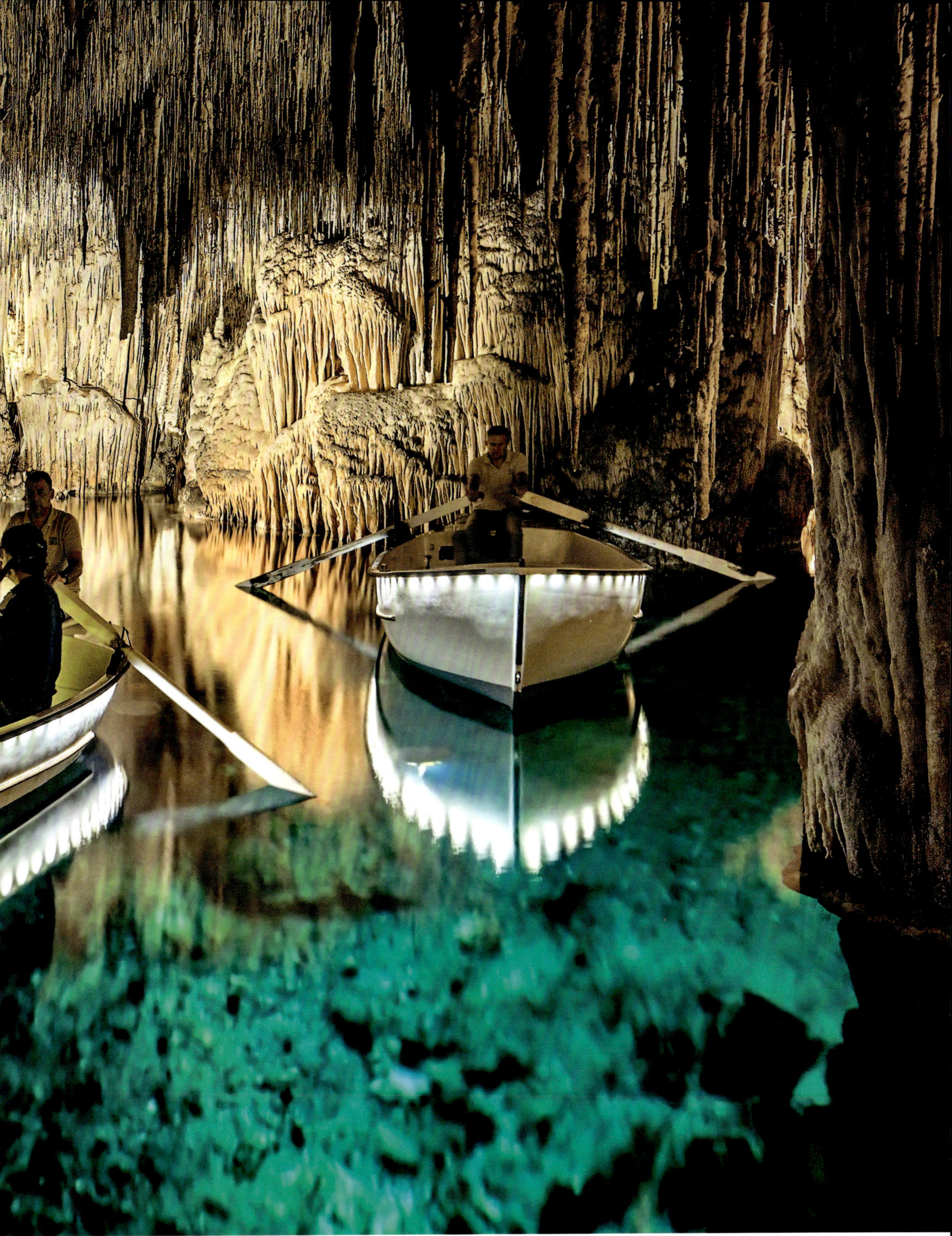

Cales de Mallorca

This is the name of the main tourist resort on the Manacor coast. It is situated between three coves —Cala Antena, which is the smallest, Es Domingos Grans and Es Domingos Petits— and is the perfect place for a family holiday.

Portocolom

The peaceful village has developed into a large natural harbour which is one of the most beautiful on the island. On the north-east tip of the bay stands the lighthouse built in 1860. Portocolom —which is known by the islanders as Es Port— still has the feel of a small fishing village and retains its seafaring spirit. It is a popular summer holiday spot for families from Felanitx, the municipality it belongs to. Portocolom is one of the few natural harbours where boats from the east of the island can shelter, and was a major centre for shipwrights, the *mestres d'aixa*, who built some of the finest examples of the boats known as *llaüts*, on the island.

S'Algar

Portocolom's most popular beach with locals and summer holidaymakers. It takes its name from the Neptune grass which grows here. Although it resembles seaweed, or algae (hence the name of the beach), it is actually a flowering plant that yields fruit. In years gone by, farmers collected it from the shore to use as compost on their crops.

S'Algar

Es Domingos

Fishermen's huts and a *llaüt* in Portocolom

Felanitx

With more than 17,000 inhabitants, the municipality is home to landmarks such as the Puig de Sant Salvador, a hill with a 14th century sanctuary and Santueri Castle perched on the top. In the late-19th century, Felanitx was a major wine producer and this was a boom time for the local economy. The wine industry is an important driver of the economy today and wine-production is thriving.

Cala Sa Nau

A lovely beach with fine, white sand at the end of a long, S-shaped inlet and bathed by waters that reflect every imaginable hue from turquoise to emerald green. There are low cliffs on either side crowned by shrubs, pines and savin junipers.

Cala Mitjana

An idyllic cove split into two narrow inlets: the one on the left extends 70 m inland while the one on the right, which is more than 100 m deep, forms a beach of white sand surrounded by cliffs with pines that back onto a housing development.

Cala Ferrera

One of the most heavily built-up beaches on this stretch of the coastline, where many Mallorcans have their second home. The large number of hotels and extensive facilities have made it into a major tourist resort that regains its calm in winter. A cliff separates it from the beautiful cove and beach, the Caló de Ses Dones.

Santueri Castle. In the background, the Sant Salvador shrine

Cala Sa Nau

Paprika

Cala Serena or Caló de Ses Dones

Migjorn

Colònia de Sant Jordi

Migjorn

The southernmost tip of Mallorca closest to Africa has a special microclimate and the cloudless sky and clear, natural light indicate that the sea isn't far away. Along the coast you'll find a succession of picture-postcard coves, such Mondragó, Cala Figuera de Santanyí and the tiny Cala de S'Almunia. Further south are some of the most beautiful unspoilt beaches on the island, such as Es Trenc, guarded on the southern edge by Ses Salines lighthouse that overlooks the Cabrera Archipelago, now a National Park. Further inland are villages that are passionate about their heritage, such as Santanyí —with its sandstone quarries— Ses Salines and Llucmajor.

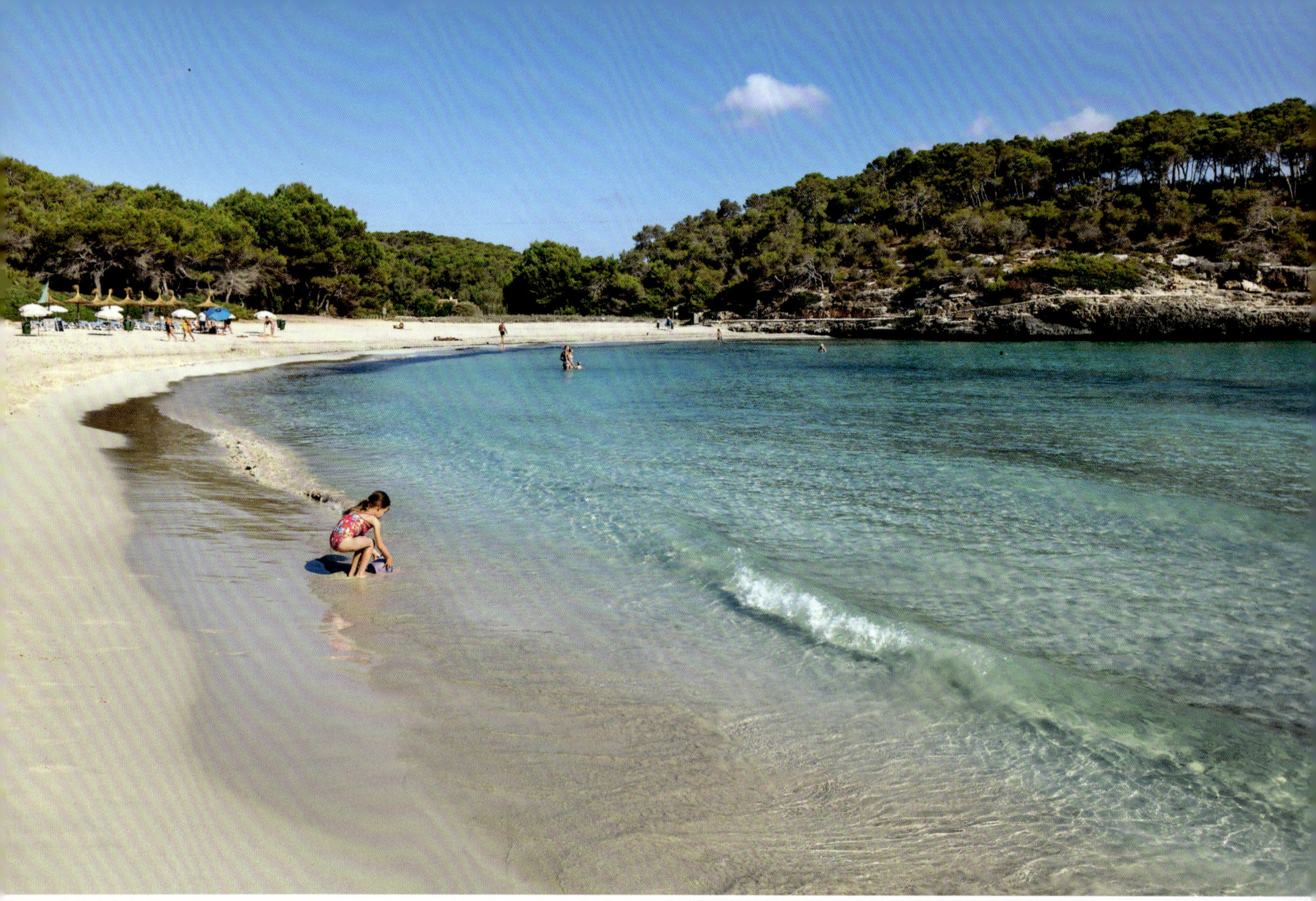
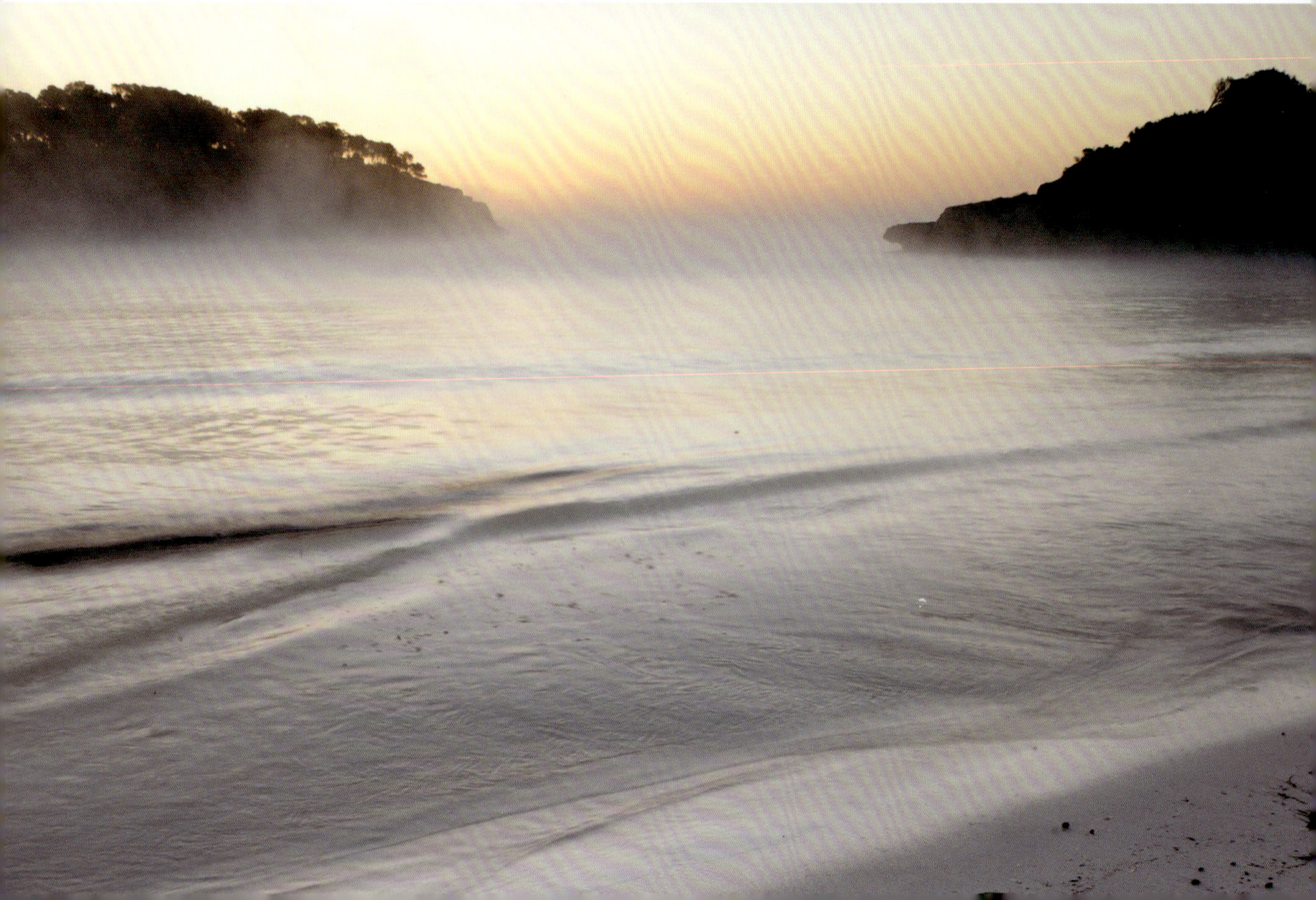

Portopetro

This old fishing harbour still retains its time-honoured charm, despite the fact that tourism is the main driver of its economy today. The beautiful, tiny bay dotted with sandy beaches is the perfect place for a stroll by the sea and you can stop off at one of the restaurants to sample the superb fresh fish brought in by the local fleet.

Parc Natural de Mondragó

This park covers an area of more than 750 ha. Only 95 are open to the public while the rest belong to private estates dedicated to dryland farming and growing crops such as almond, carob and fig trees and grains. For centuries, agriculture and livestock farming have left their mark on the Mondragó landscape where you can still see characteristic features such as drystone walls, huts, terraces, charcoal furnaces, lime kilns, water wheels, dikes, pools and cisterns. The landscape mostly consists of scrubland with botanical gems such as a wide variety of orchid species. Birdlife includes mallards, moorhens, common coots and herons which frequent the brackish ponds that form at the ends of the torrents of S'Amarador and Fonts de N'Alis.

Santanyí

Throughout the island there are buildings made of sandstone from the Santanyí quarries. The stone has been exported to France and Italy and has also been used to build many of the houses and other buildings in the town, such as the church of Sant Andreu, which houses a valuable baroque organ. Every Saturday the town is buzzing with activity when it holds its weekly market. Craftspeople, growers and artists from across the island come here to sell their wares. Santanyí has a large foreign population, mostly from Germany, who run some of the restaurants, shops and art galleries.

↖ S'Amarador
← Cala Mondragó

Portopetro

Traditional houses in Santanyí

Cala Figuera de Santanyí

One of the most unique and harmonious landscapes on the south-east coast: a sea inlet with a mouth that it is 100 m wide which narrows to form two branches that make up the Caló d'En Busques and Caló d'En Boira. This is one of the longest, narrowest and most sheltered formations on the Balearic Islands.

Cala Santanyí

From this tourist beach, nestling among low cliffs, you can walk as far as Es Pontàs, a natural rock formation in the shape of an arch which has become a landmark along this stretch of the coastline. The cove with its white sands and transparent waters is popular with surfers and scuba divers.

Cala Figuera

Es Pontàs

Santanyí **Migjorn**

Cala Llombards
The mouth of the Son Amer torrent forms this deep cove with its white, sandy beach that backs onto a pine forest. It has a family atmosphere and is popular with summer holidaymakers from the surrounding holiday complexes. On the left-hand side of the beach there are a number of fisherman's huts that blend into the scenery.

Cala S'Almunia
A lovely cove where there is barely enough room to spread out your towel. There is a landing stage cut out of the rock by the sea and the wind, which has ramps for boats to enter the water. From the shore you can see the tiny cove of Es Caló des Moro with its small sandy beach and crystal-clear waters.

Cala S'Almunia

Cala Llombards

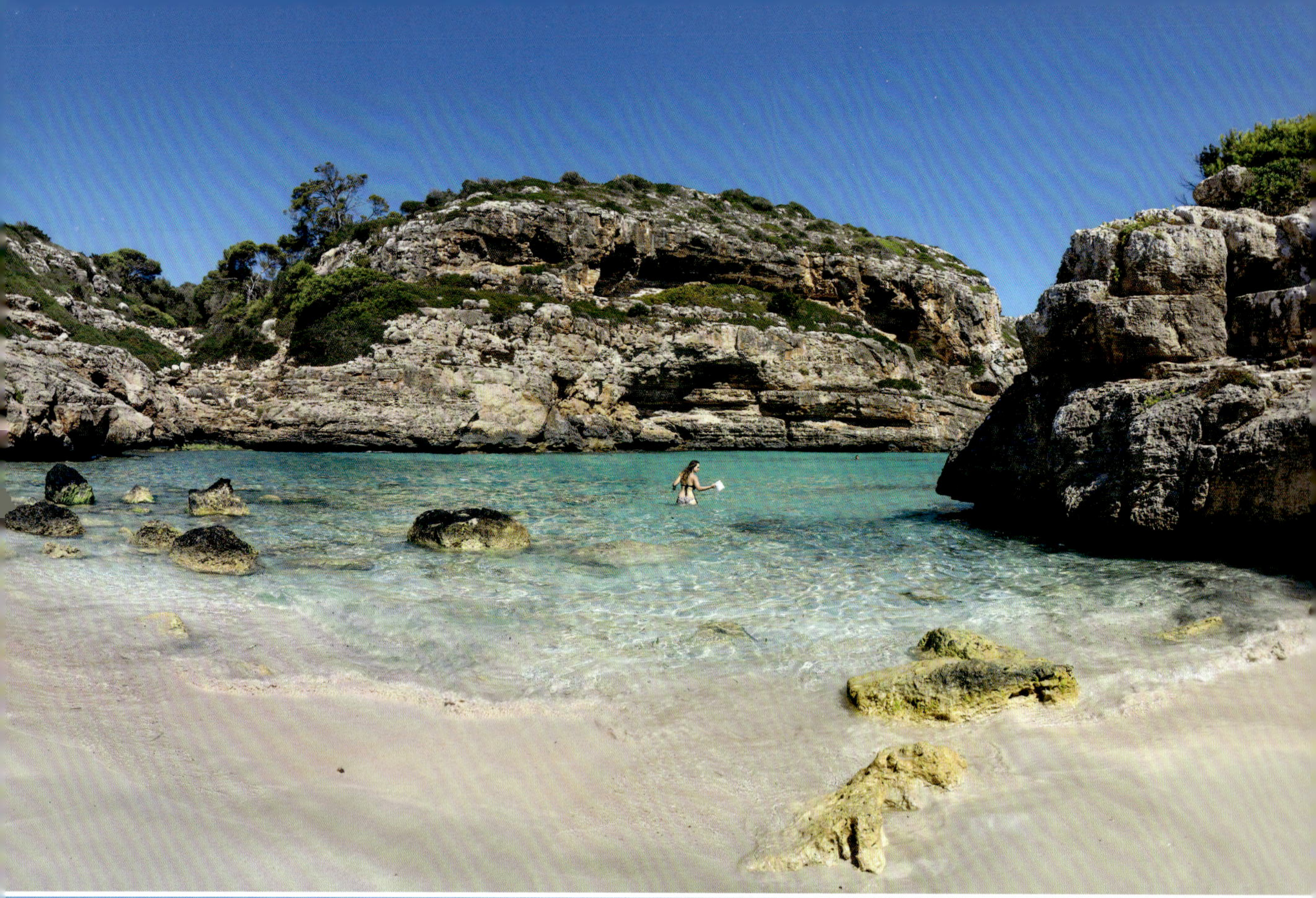

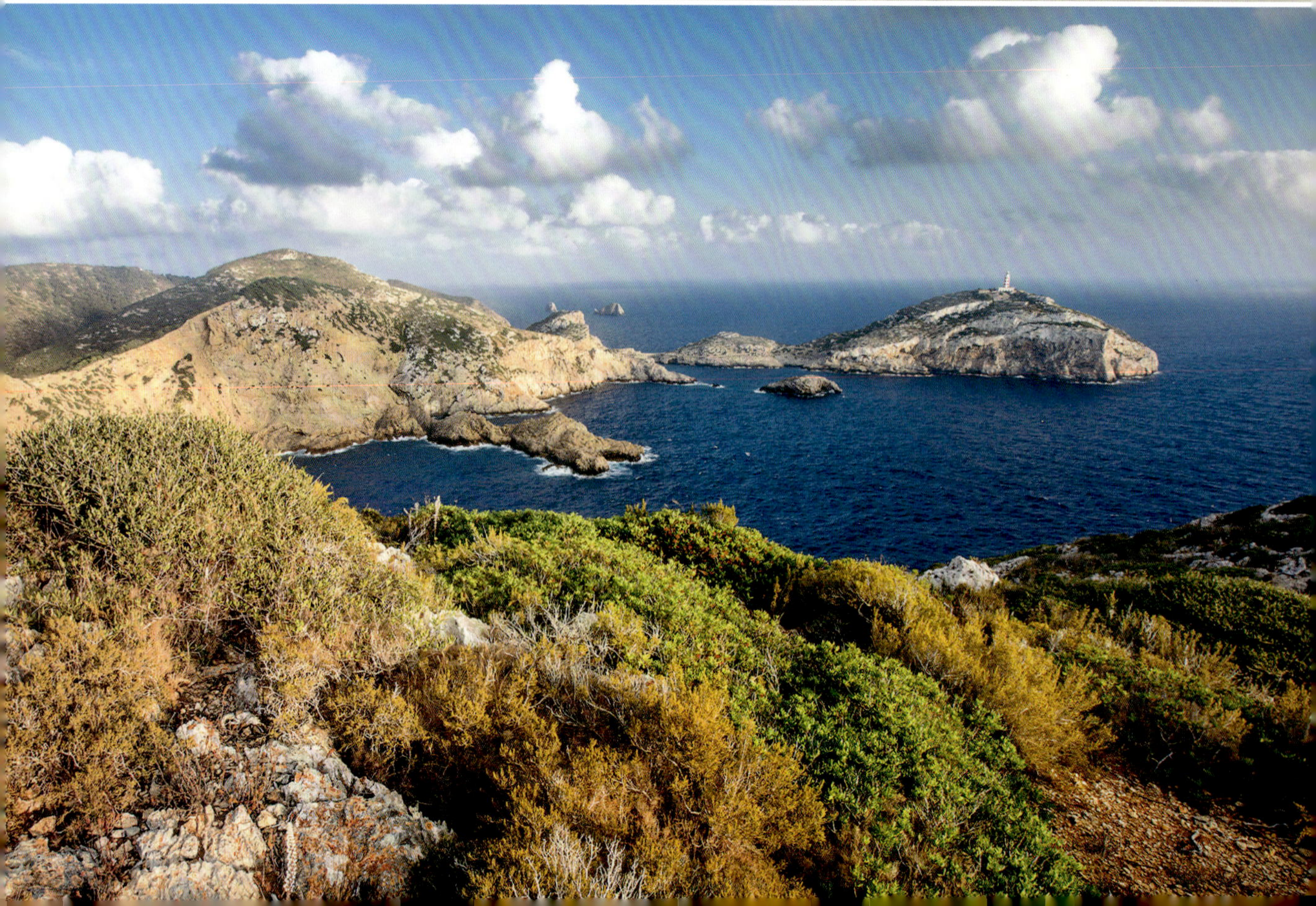

Reserva Marina de Migjorn

This marine reserve stands on a wide inland strip between Cap Blanc, Cap de ses Salines and Cala Figuera de Santanyí. It covers an area of 22,332 ha. Most of the seabed is sandy and is home to vast meadows of *Posidonia oceanica*, or Neptune grass, where a whole host of species find refuge, food and a place to breed. Neptune grass is a marine plant that is endemic to the Mediterranean. Just like plants that grow on dry land, it has roots and a stem. Its distinctive feature are its ribbon-shaped leaves that grow up to 1 m in length. Neptune grass has many beneficial properties: it protects the coast from erosion and is considered an indicator of the quality of the sea water.

Cap de Ses Salines

Parc Nacional Marítimoterrestre de Cabrera

This park stands 10 nautical miles from Colònia de Sant Jordi. It covers an area of more than 10,000 ha, 8,703 of which correspond to the marine environment and the remainder to the 18 islands and islets that make up the Cabrera Archipelago. It is a place steeped in history: in the 19th century, its castle was used a concentration camp for almost 9,000 French prisoners, most of whom perished. Today it is a peaceful spot with a wealth of flora and fauna and rich in endemic species, including ten subspecies of Lilford's wall lizard (*Podarcis lilfordi*), beetles, spiders and snails. Its waters, with their rocky and sandy beds, are home to groupers, starfish and dolphins, and seabirds can be spotted on the surface.

Cabrera Castle

↖ Caló des Màrmols
← Cabrera. N'Ensiola lighthouse

Ses Salines

Peace and quiet pervade this village, near the salt flats of Es Trenc and Sa Vall, and many foreigners choose to live here because it provides convenient access to the beaches in the south. The area has been inhabited for centuries, and the pre-historic sites, such as Els Antigors, and Roman sites, like the necropolis of Sa Carrotja, bear witness to this fact. Most of the buildings are made from sandstone. These include the church of Sant Bartomeu, which was built between 1876 and 1955 to a design by Pere d'Alcàntara Penya. This place of worship replaced the tiny 17th-century parish church, which is still standing.

Colònia de Sant Jordi

Colònia de Sant Jordi was once a fishing village where a defence tower, now vanished, once stood. From 1879 onwards, an agricultural settlement established itself here inhabited by workers from the salt flats and adjacent farmsteads. At the start of the 20th century, Mallorcan families began to buy their second homes here and it then grew into a tourist destination. There is seafront promenade which is perfect for sports lovers and a great place for a stroll by the sea with the ever-present outline of the Cabrera Archipelago on the horizon. Boats bound for the Parc Nacional de Cabrera depart from its tiny harbour, which is packed with traditional craft, known as *llaüts*, and leisure boats.

Ses Salines. Church of Sant Bartomeu

Botanicactus

Colònia de Sant Jordi

Ses Salines | Colònia de Sant Jordi **Migjorn**

Es Carbó and Es Dolç

The unspoilt coastline that links up the beautiful beaches in the south of Mallorca stretches to the east of Colònia de Sant Jordi. You can only get to Es Carbó on foot or by boat. With the island of Na Moltona standing guard over the bay, Es Carbó is an almost-deserted spot which merges with the popular Es Dolç beach, which is frequented by summer holidaymakers in the area.

Salines de Sa Vall and Salines des Trenc

The Salines de Sa Vall, where sea salt is still harvested, are among the oldest salt flats in the Mediterranean. Salt is first thought to have been gathered here by the Phoenicians between the 4th and 2nd centuries AD. Nearby, are the Salines des Trenc, where salt is extracted for industrial and culinary uses. It specialises in *fleur du sel*, which is the purest and richest in trace elements. It forms crystals on the surface of the salt pans.

Salines de Sa Vall

Es Dolç beach

↑ Es Trenc ↓ Es Salobrar de Campos

Es Trenc
One of the few beaches on the island with no buildings around it. It has fine, white sand and extends inland to form a valuable dune system that separates the beach from a wetland area where sea salt is harvested. More than 170 bird species have been identified in the wetlands where they stop off to feed and rest during their migrations. Es Trenc is also a symbol of the local ecology movement which has managed to put a stop to a number of building projects in the area.

The Salobrar de Campos
A protected wetland area and a Natural Area of Special Interest that includes Es Trenc beach, a dune ridge and the natural and artificial lakes used for salt production. It is a popular spot for bird watchers who come here to see the birds that feed, rest or nest in the area.

Ses Covetes
A white, sandy beach with crystal-clear waters and a laid-back atmosphere that is popular with the islanders. There are prehistoric burial chambers nearby as well as the only thermal springs on Mallorca.

Sa Ràpita
A peaceful spot popular with summer holidaymakers that has established itself around the beautiful Sa Ràpita beach with its fine, white sand. It is also renowned for its many restaurants that specialise in rice, fish and seafood dishes.

Ses Covetes

Windmills in Campos

Salt flats in Es Salobrar de Campos

↑ **Cala Pi tower**   ↓ **Cala Blava**

Llucmajor **Migjorn**

Sa Marina de Llucmajor
This stretch of the coastline is situated between S'Estanyol de Migjorn and Cap Enderrocat. Part of it has been declared a Natural Area of Special Interest. The coast is lined with cliffs and is fairly inaccessible, with bathing areas including Es Davallador des Carros.

Cap Blanc
A cape that encloses the Bay of Palma to the east. An isolated spot buffeted by the wind and the waves which is part of the protected area of Sa Marina de Llucmajor. Around it there are miles and miles of roads that are popular with cyclists.

Cala Mosques or Cala Blava
Cala Blava is a quiet resort where the locals value their proximity to the city of Palma and easy access to small, family-friendly coves such as Cala Mosques. Well-kept secrets which can sometimes only be reached by steps.

Capocorb Vell
This is one of the most important, largest and best-preserved prehistoric settlements on Mallorca. There are five talayots —towers built with large irregular blocks of masonry, known as the cyclopean technique— as well as the outline of several dwellings.

Cap Blanc

Garriga

Capocorb Vell

The interior
Tramuntana interior, El Raiguer and El Pla

The Serra de Tramuntana seen from El Raiguer

The interior: Tramuntana interior, El Raiguer and El Pla

The interior of the island consists of vast areas of land dotted with villages which best preserve the island's traditions, gastronomy and architectural heritage, with a plethora of churches and convents, as well as chapels and sanctuaries that stand on low-lying hills. It is the agricultural and livestock larder which supplies the weekly open-air markets with produce. The main producers of wine, olive oil, almonds, cured sausage made from the black pig, figs and apricots are to be found here and you can sample their wares at the *cellers*, old wineries that have now become bastions of traditional cuisine.

Tramuntana interior

Puigpunyent, Orient, Esporles and Bunyola are towns nestling among some of the most beautiful scenery on the Serra de Tramuntana. Their proximity to Palma means that their population has grown considerably in recent years. Picture-postcard villages surrounded by mountains, with steeply sloping terrain that requires stepped streets to make them more accessible. They are criss-crossed by paths which overlook old charcoal furnaces and lime kilns that provide proof of the exploitation of woodland resources. There are also a number of private estates, now open to the public, with stately gardens, such as Raixa and Alfàbia, which can be visited.

Alfàbia Gardens

Orient

The interior: Tramuntana interior, El Raiguer and El Pla

El Raiguer

This county, in the north-central part of Mallorca, follows the contours of the Serra de Tramuntana, and includes the municipalities of Alaró, Binissalem, Búger, Campanet, Consell, Lloseta, Mancor de la Vall, Marratxí, Sa Pobla, Santa Maria del Camí and Selva. Towns that overlook the mountains that have harnessed woodland resources for centuries, mainly to obtain charcoal, lime, wild mushrooms, firewood and game. You can still see plots of farmland planted with vines, almond and olive trees connected by a network of paths and winding roads that are popular with hikers and cyclists.

Inca is the capital of El Raiguer and is the third-largest town on the island in terms of population, after Palma and Manacor. For centuries it has been a major centre for the production of leather goods and is home to world-renowned footwear brands. Every Thursday the town holds a huge open-air market,

Alaró Castle

Caimari olive tree

which epitomises its enterprising spirit, and in November people from all over the island come to the largest annual fair, Dijous Bo. Its provides a showcase for farmers, wine-makers and craftspeople from the island and the events include livestock auctions and competitions of local breeds. There is a wide variety of food stalls.

In the past, wine-making was one of the main industries on this part of the island, a fact borne out by the presence of old wineries, known as *cellers*, many of which have been converted into restaurants. Wine-production has undergone a renaissance in recent years, and the quality designation, Denominación de Origen Binissalem, identifies the wines produced in this area with native grape varieties and traditional techniques. Excellent wines are also made from other grape blends. Every September, the town of Binissalem marks the grape harvest with a week-long celebration, the *Festes des Vermar*, which features all kinds of events associated with the world of wine. All the local wineries attend to present their new wines.

The Festes de Sant Antoni are one of the most popular festivals on the island. The village of Sa Pobla hosts one of the best known and most spectacular. On the night of 17th January, the villagers light large bonfires, or *foguerons*, in the street, they share food and drink and the devil and the saint engage in mock battles between good and evil. At midnight the poets, or *glossadors*, make up verses by the bonfire, while the people eat the typical *espinagades*, pasties filled with vegetables and pork loin or eel.

One of the paths on the GR-221, the *Ruta de la Pedra en Sec*

Museu del Calçat, Inca

Selva

↑ Raixa   ↓ *Celler*, restaurant serving traditional cuisine, in Inca

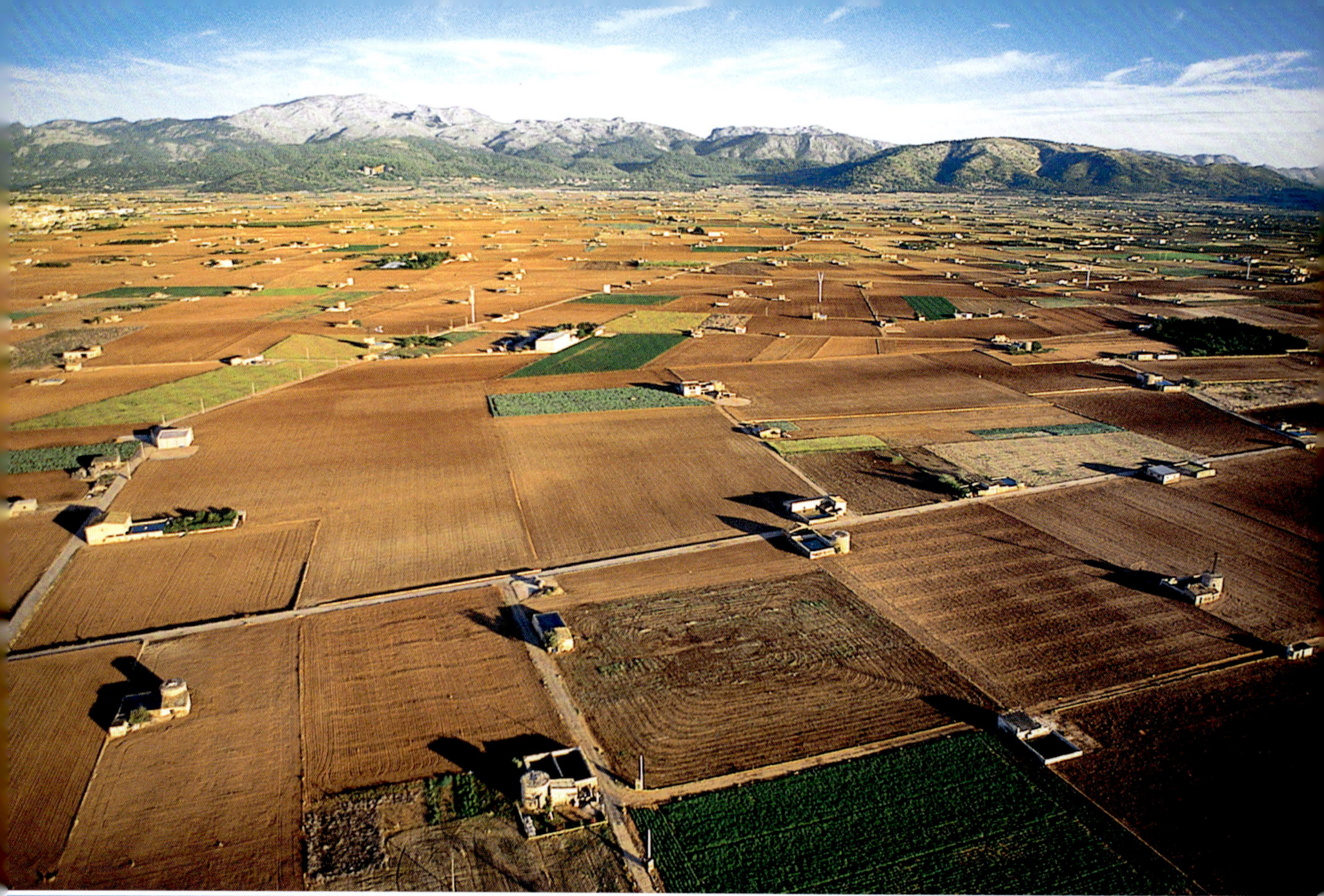

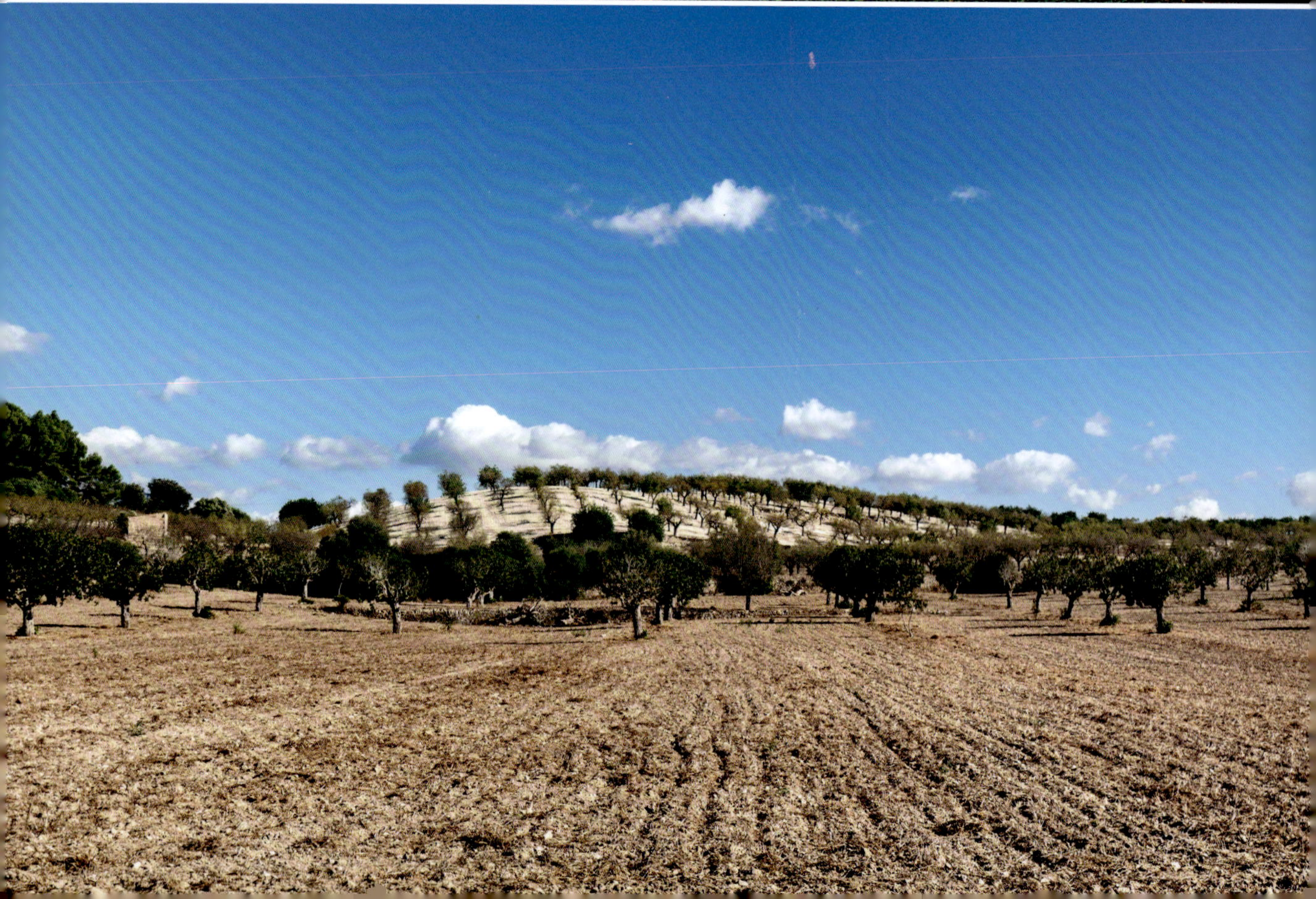

El Pla

Mallorca's central county El Pla (the plain), lies in a depression formed by the mountain ranges of the Serra de Tramuntana and Serres de Llevant. It includes the municipalities of Algaida, Ariany, Costitx, Lloret de Vistalegre, Llubí, Maria de la Salut, Montuïri, Petra, Porreres, Santa Eugènia, Sant Joan, Sencelles, Sineu and Vilafranca de Bonany, which are firmly rooted in the landscape and farming. In spite of its name, this is not in fact a completely flat plateau. It is dotted with hills, often crowned by chapels or sanctuaries, that boast beautiful panoramic views.

El Pla covers an area of 600 km² and accounts for 21.56% of the island's surface. Most of the land stands between 50 and 150 m above sea level, and its highest peak is Puig de Randa (548 m). El Pla is criss-crossed by torrents that flow out into the Bay of Alcúdia, in S'Albufera and the Bay of Palma. The natural vegetation consists of holm oak, pine and wild olive groves which are mostly found in the hills of Randa, Son Seguí, Bonany, Sant Miquel and Sant Nofre, the woodland area of La Comuna de Lloret and the environs of the Na Borges torrent, which are all areas of outstanding natural beauty.

For centuries, farming was the main economic activity in this inland area and has shaped the landscape we see today. The land is still planted with

Sineu

Prickly pears

↖ **Farmland in Sa Pobla**
← **Outskirts of Montuïri**

Sencelles

cereals, fruit trees and crops for fodder which are sold at the markets in Palma and throughout the island. Many buildings and structures still stand bearing witness to the rural life of the past. These include mills, cisterns, wells, drystone walls that demarcate the plots of land, and *possessions*, estates devoted to farming and livestock raising, many of which became self-sufficient. Many of the *possessions* have been converted into rural B & Bs. The paths and minor roads around them are popular with hikers and cyclists from all over the world.

All the villages in El Pla have a similar layout: stone houses clustered around the church, which was the first building to be constructed in the village. Since the time of the Christian conquest, in the 13th century, the church wielded the greatest influence on local traditions and village life. Many of the festivities have a religious basis and, architecturally speaking, the church was the most important building, with its own historic and artistic value. Other structures, such as wayside crosses, rectories, convents, sanctuaries and chapels bear witness to the influence of religion on society.

El Pla has been inhabited since prehistoric times, as borne out by the archaeological remains dating from the second millennium AD. The talayots are the main manifestation of the presence of early cultures in the area. These defence towers were built using cyclopean techniques consisting of large irregular blocks of masonry. There are

Noble coat of arms on a façade

Carriage

Montuïri

↑ Algaida ↓ Petra

Picking almonds

The characteristic green of the doors and shutters on Mallorca

a number of important talayotic sites on this part of the island, including the settlement of Son Fornés, at Montuïri, and the sanctuary of Son Corró de Costitx. Two bronze bull heads were found at Son Corró, unique pieces that are the ultimate expression of the worship of this animal.

Sineu is the county capital, a historic town where the kings of Mallorca, Jaume II and Sanç, established their residence outside the city. The 16th century Gothic church of Santa Maria is the most important landmark. A winged lion stands guard outside, the symbol of Saint Mark, the local patron saint. The surrounding streets have imposing mansions and centuries-old buildings such as the Conceptionist convent, which was the former palace of King Jaume II. The town bursts into life every Wednesday when it holds is huge weekly market, which was first documented in 1252. There are hundreds of stalls selling clothes, animals, accessories, local produce and handcrafted goods.

The villages in the county usually hold their traditional fairs between autumn and spring. This is one of the best times to visit and discover the excellent local foods and handcrafted goods. The fairs usually focus on an iconic local product. For instance, Porreres hosts the Fira de l'Albercoc (apricot), Vilafranca de Bonany holds the Fira del Meló (melon) and Llubí is home to the Fira de la Mel (honey).

El Pla is also home to some of the most important festivals on the island. This is largely due to the fact that the inland areas have preserved their centuries-old traditions better than anywhere else on Mallorca. The dance of the *cossiers* is a central event of the festivals at Montuïri —held on 24th August, Saint Bartholomew's Day— and Algaida, where the *cossiers* dance on 16th January, Saint Honoratus' Day. The *cossiers* are among the most unusual and mysterious characters who take part in the festivals. Six men and one lady dressed in white and wearing coloured sashes perform ancient dances while the devil tries to interrupt them with his tricks. These

The interior: Tramuntana interior, El Raiguer and El Pla

Porreres

Monti-sion shrine

Examples of the native black pig

Santa Maria del Camí

dances are thought to originate with the Catalan settlers who came to the island in the 13th century, although they may date from an earlier time. In the dance, the lady stands for good and the devil represents evil, while the *cossiers* are there to support and protect the lady. In summer, the villages in the area hold street parties, known as *verbenes*, that fill the night with music and dancing.

Gastronomy is also well represented in El Pla. Most of the villages have *cellers*, former wineries that have been converted into restaurants serving traditional cuisine. They are a favourite haunt of the locals at weekends, and are the best place to discover local dishes, such as *frit* —a fry-up of finely chopped potatoes, vegetables and sheep or pig offal seasoned with spices— or roast suckling pig with potatoes, which is usually the centrepiece of special celebrations.

Wine also plays an important role and has been produced here since Roman times. The quality designation, Denominació d'Origen Pla i Llevant, identifies the wines produced in the area, and you will often come across vast expanses of vineyards and wineries, many of them open to visitors.

Petra and the Serres de Llevant from the Bonany shrine ↗
Market at Maria de la Salut →

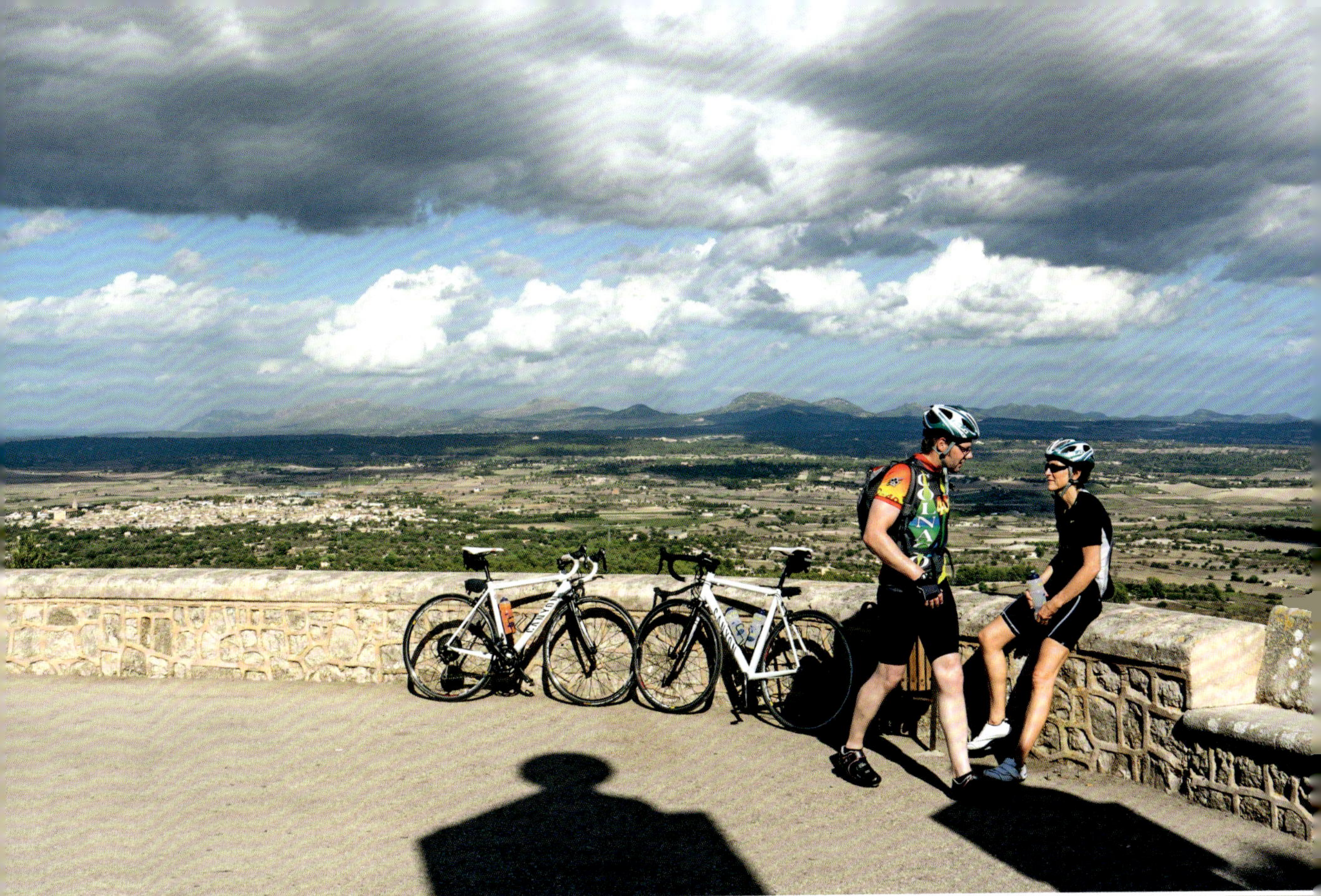

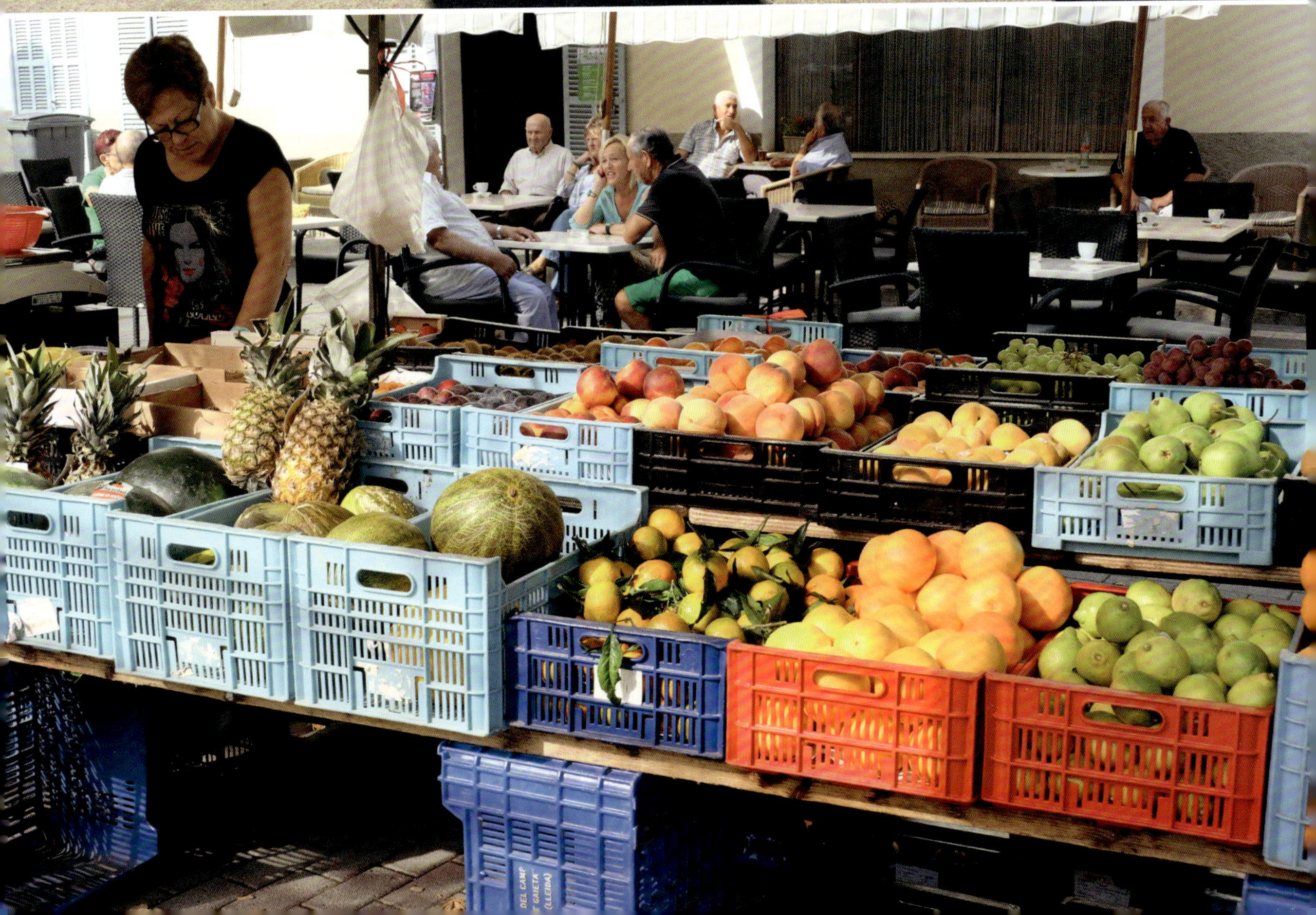

Gastronomy

Mallorcan cuisine is based on local ingredients, such as pork from the black pig, lamb, fish, seasonal vegetables, and locally produced olive oil and wine. They form the basis of a vast repertoire of recipes that includes time-consuming dishes, such as *frit*. The island is particularly renowned for its cakes and pastries, and has a plethora of savoury flatbreads and cakes —such as vegetable pasties, *cocarrois*, and meat pasties, *panades*— and a sweet empire where the spiral pastry, the *ensaïmada*, reigns supreme, followed by specialities such as *crespell* biscuits, and pasties, known as *doblegats* and *robiols*. Mallorcan wines are becoming more and more highly regarded and the island has been awarded two quality designations of origin: D.O. Pla i Llevant and D.O. Binissalem.

Sobrassada
On Mallorca, the pig is viewed as a true "benefactor" and every part is used, from snout to tail. This soft sausage is made from the finest meat with a generous handful of paprika. It is often spread on bread or added to traditional dishes.

Time-honoured shops
Markets and small grocery shops select the finest produce from the island: extra-virgin olive oil, wine, cured meats and sausage, oranges, apricots, jam and essential spices such as paprika.

Pa amb oli
A Mallorcan staple. A simple dish consisting of slices of bread, preferably brown, spread with tomato, drizzled with virgin olive oil and sprinkled with salt. It is eaten with local cheeses, cured meats and sausage, cracked olives and wine.

Gastronomy

Sopes mallorquines
Finely sliced dry brown bread is placed in a casserole dish and a hearty vegetable soup, to which meat or wild mushrooms may be added, is poured over it. The bread soaks up all the liquid to create this rustic favourite.

Tumbet
A favourite summer recipe combining aubergine, red pepper and potato, fried separately and covered in tomato sauce. It is eaten on its own or as a garnish for meat and fish dishes.

Ensaïmada
The emblem of the island's bakeries and an iconic food. The secret of the velvety texture of this spiral pastry lies in the use of lard, or *saïm*, hence its name.

Greixonera
A dessert that is a perennial favourite at traditional restaurants. It takes its name from the earthenware casserole, or *greixonera*, it is made in. The ingredients: an ensaimada from the previous day to form the base, sugar, eggs, cinnamon, lemon and curd cheese.

Handicrafts

Handcrafted goods are not just thriving, they are currently being reappraised and young designers are using traditional materials, including fabrics, such as *teles de llengos*, and esparto grass to create their new pieces. In summer, the late-night, open-air markets in the coastal villages showcase the work of goldsmiths, silversmiths, potters, ceramicists, carpenters, basket makers and glass blowers. During the rest of the year, you can buy unique handmade products at the many craft fairs around the island. Made from sustainable materials they are extremely durable. Many craftspeople open their studios in inspiring towns such as Artà, Pòrtol, Sóller, Pollença and Sineu.

Tela de llengos
These fabrics are made using a millennia-old technique known as *ikat*, which consists of dying fabrics using a resist process. The fabric is woven by hand and used to make curtains, bedspreads and cushions and to upholster sofas and rocking chairs.

Siurell
Ancestral clay whistle in the form of a human, devil or animal that some historians relate to Minoan-Cretan ceramics. The traditional ones are painted white with green and red lines on top.

Blown glass
A centuries-old tradition whereby the glass blower gathers a gobbet of molten glass on the end of an iron rod and blows through the other end while shaping the glass with tongs to achieve the desired shape. Glasses, vases and lamps are made using this technique.

Handicrafts

Basket making
The dried leaves of the palmetto palm are used to weave baskets, saddlebags, mats and other useful and beautiful utensils. An ancestral technique, traditionally the domain of women, which is associated with the towns of Artà and Capdepera in particular.

Olive wood
The olive tree is not only a source of oil and olives. Its durable, silky-smooth wood is used to make household utensils such as spatulas, bowls, pestles and mortars as well as sculptures.

Potteries
Pòrtol and Sa Cabaneta are the centre of Mallorca's pottery industry. Numerous potters have their studios here where they make earthenware casseroles, crockery, tiles, *siurell* whistles and other beautiful clay objects using centuries-old techniques.

Leather and footwear
The Shoemakers' Guild has been one of the most important on the island since the 13th century. Inca is particularly renowned for its shoes. It is currently the home of a number of world-famous footwear brands.

Traditions

The calendar is packed with festivals and traditions dating back hundreds of years. The seaside towns and villages hold processions on the day of Our Lady of Carmen, the patron saint of sailors. Further inland there are festivals where dancing devils and bonfires take centre stage. These include Sant Antoni, which takes place at the height of summer, and Sant Joan, in early summer. In places such as Pollença and Sóller, all the townspeople take to the streets to stage mock battles between Moors and Christians. Some of the festivals centre on local characters, like Santa Catalina Tomàs, and others involve *cossiers* (six men and one lady who dance to ancient tunes), *gegants* (giant figures with a painted papier-mâché head and body), and *capgrossos* (figures with oversized papier-mâché heads). During the summer, street parties fill the nights on the island with music and revelry.

The *cossiers*

Six men and a lady dressed in white perform ancestral dances to the sound of traditional instruments, such as a small drum known as a *tamborí* and the woodwind *flabiol*. They are accompanied by a devil who tries to interrupt the dance.

Blauets from Lluc

This children's choir, known as *blauets* because of the blue cassocks they wear, is the oldest musical formation on Mallorca. Founded in the 16th century, they sing daily at the Sanctuary of Lluc.

Trotting races

The racecourses in Palma and Manacor hold these thrilling races. The horses are hitched to a lightweight buggy and trot along guided by skilful jockeys. A thrilling sport that will make you tingle with excitement.

Traditions

Moors and Christians
Sóller and Pollença stage a mock battle between Moors and Christians during their local festival which the entire town takes part in. Centuries ago, pirate raids were common and these battles commemorate the islanders who risked life and limb to protect their towns and villages.

Santa Catalina Tomàs
Mallorca's most popular saint, better known as the *beateta*. She was born in Valldemossa in the 16th century and, in July, the town holds the Festes de la Beata in her honour. The town of Santa Margalida also pays tribute to Santa Catalina at its festival in September.

Mallorcan *rondalles*
Traditional Mallorcan folk tales that have been passed down orally from generation to generation. At some festivals, characters from these tales appear as *gegants* and *capgrossos*.

Sant Antoni
In January, many towns and villages on the island celebrate the Festes de Sant Antoni, which symbolise Saint Anthony's struggle with the devil who roams the streets. A festival with a profusion of bonfires and performances by local poets, particularly in Sa Pobla and Artà.

Published by
© Triangle Postals

Text
© Marga Font

© Photography
Ricard Pla, p. 7b, 18, 26a, 38b, 54b, 58b, 59b, 81a, 83ab, 85b, 90b, 91ab, 94a, 96a, 99a, 102b, 103ac, 108b, 109d, 121ac, 123c, 132a, 135a;
Biel Puig, p. 22a, 46, 48ab, 49bc, 51a, 52ab, 53ab, 55, 57a, 58a, 59a, 61a, 70bc, 71ab, 72a, 76bc, 77ab, 79b, 80a, 84b, 95bc, 96bc, 97b, 99b, 100, 102c, 104b, 105ab, 106, 108c, 112a, 113b, 114ab, 115b, 116a, 121b, 122b, cober;
Oleguer Farriol, p. 2, 4, 6, 9ab, 11ab, 16ab, 17b, 20d, 22b, 31b, 44a, 45c, 54a, 57b, 60, 62a, 70a, 72b, 81c, 82a, 88, 104c, 109b, 117a, 119b, 120a, 122a, 124, 128c; **Hans Hansen**, p. 7a, 8a, 21b, 23a, 30b, 31a, 32a, 34b, 35a, 38a, 39a, 40a, 49a, 51b, 64a, 108a, 110, 115a, 118ac, 126b, 127b, 128a, 129b, 131c, 132b, 134ab, 141d; **Sebastià Torrens**, p. 40b, 64b, 66abc, 67ab, 73a, 78, 79ab, 86, 87ab, 92ab, 93, 95a, 112b, 116b, 117b, 120b, 123ab, 128b, 142ab, 143d; **Joan Colomer**, p. 8b, 14ab, 15b, 17a, 19ab, 20ac, 21ad, 23b, 26c, 30a, 62b, 81b, 84a, 85ac, 90a, 94bc, 104a, 130b, 131a, 132c, 133ab, 136b, 137ab, 140abc, 141abc, 143bc; **Laia Moreno**, p. 15a, 23c, 32b, 33ab, 34a, 42, 43ab, 44b, 45ab, 63ab, 68, 73b, 74, 76a, 82b, 98, 99c, 109c, 113a, 126a, 129a, 131b, 138a; **Pere Vivas**, p. 10, 12ab, 13ab, 20b, 21c, 24, 25, 26b, 27;
Juanjo Puente, p. 28, 35b, 36, 39b, 103b, 118b, 119a, 135b;
Jordi Todó, p. 56, 61b, 80b, 105c; **Oriol Aleu**, p. 97a, 109a, 136a, 138bc, 139abcd; **Neil Austen**, p. 50ab, 127a, 130a; **Toni Salas**, p. 143a;
Colau Forteza, p. 142c; **Sergi Escandell**, p. 102a

Art Direction
Ricard Pla

Graphic design
Joan Colomer

Translation
Steve Cedar

Printed by
Gongraf

Registration number
Me 154-2016

ISBN
978-84-8478-692-4

Printed in Barcelona, 5/2023

TRIANGLE POSTALS, SL
Sant Lluís
Menorca
Tel. +34 971 15 04 51
www.triangle.cat

This book may not be reproduced totally or partially by any means, including reprography and computerised treatment, without the written authorisation of the copyright holders.

Triangle▸Books

www.triangle.cat